W9-BZT-266

Physical Characteristics of the Lhasa Apso

(from the American Kennel Club breed standard)

Body Shape: The length from point of shoulders to point of buttocks longer than height at withers, well ribbed up, strong loin, well-developed quarters and thighs.

Tail and Carriage: Well feathered, should be carried well over back in a screw; there may be a kink at the end.

Size: Variable, but about 10 inches or 11 inches at shoulder for dogs, bitches slightly smaller.

Color: All colors equally acceptable with or without dark tips to ears and beard.

Coat: Heavy, straight, hard, not woolly nor silky, of good length, and very dense.

Feet: Well feathered, should be round and catlike, with good pads.

Lhasa Apso

By Juliette Cunliffe

Contents

KENNEL CLUB BOOKS® LHASA APSO
ISBN: 1-59378-218-7

Copyright © 2003, **2006** • Kennel Club Books, LLC
308 Main Street, Allenhurst, NJ 07711 USA
Cover Design Patented: US 6,435,559 B2 • Printed in South Korea

10 9 8 7 6 5 4 3

Photography by Carol Ann Johnson,
with additional photographs by:

Norvia Behling, Carolina Biological Supply, Liza Clancy,
Juliette Cunliffe, Doskocil, Isabelle Francais, James Hayden-Yoav,
James R. Hayden, RBP, Dwight R. Kuhn, Dr. Dennis Kunkel,
Mikki Pet Products, Antonio Phillipe, Phototake, Jean Claude Revy,
Samsung, Dr. Andrew Spielman and C. James Webb.

Illustrations by Patricia Peters

The publisher wishes to thank all of the owners of the dogs featured in this book,
including Madame Annie Bondier, Wendy Cain, Juliette Cunliffe, Lynne Horton,
Carol Ann Johnson, Anne Lyttle, Jean Stropko and RoseAnn Tilton.

History of the
LHASA APSO

The enchanting little Lhasa Apso, considered by his admirers to be a big dog in a small body, hails from Tibet, the land known as "The Roof of the World." This mystical country with its barren landscape lies at a high altitude. Inhabitants, both human and canine, have to be able to deal with extremes of temperature and fiercely bright light. The Tibetans are a stalwart race, and truly typical Apsos carry many traits similar to those of their original owners.

The Lhasa Apso is said to have existed since 800 B.C., but there is no tangible evidence of this as written historical records in Tibet were not kept until around A.D. 639. Buddhism spread from India into Tibet during the seventh century. In this faith, the lion, in its various mythological forms, plays an important part. Indeed the Buddha Manjusri, the god of learning, is believed to travel around as a simple priest with a small dog. This dog, although not an Apso, can instantly be transformed into a lion so that the Buddha can ride on its back.

It is the snow lion, though, that is considered the king of animals and it is with this white

Conjuring images of the mythical lion, today's Lhasa Apso possesses all the nobility and pride of the great cat of the jungle, though he is considerably easier to live with.

mythological beast that the Lhasa Apso is most closely connected. The snow lion is believed to be so powerful that when it roars seven dragons fall out of the sky.

Lhasa Apsos have sometimes been said to be sacred animals, but this is not so. They were certainly kept in monasteries, primarily to give a warning bark to the monks if ever intruders or uninvited guests managed to get past the enormous Tibetan Mastiffs tethered outside. Nonetheless, the breed was held in high esteem. The dogs historically never were sold, but only given as gifts, for Lhasa Apsos were

Opposite page: The author and one of her Apsos, posing as the noble snow lion.

Tibetan Spaniels with their pet cat.

believed to carry the souls of monks who erred in their previous lives. Such dogs were also given as tribute gifts for safe passage from Tibet to China, a long journey by caravan that took eight to ten months.

Although Tibetans have always drawn a distinction between the "true" lion and the "dog" lion, they have never been too clear about the naming of their breeds. Without doubt, some crossing took place between the various Tibetan breeds. Even today it is possible to breed together two full-coated Lhasa Apsos and to produce one or more puppies that look like pure-bred Tibetan Spaniels. This may come as something of a shock, but is clearly a throwback to earlier days. Interestingly, the Tibetans refer to all long-coated dogs as "Apsok," which further complicates matters when trying to research the history of Tibetan breeds.

APSO SENG KYI

The breed has been known as "Apso Seng Kyi," which has been translated as "Bark Sentinel Lion Dog." However, the author considers a more accurate translation to be "hairy mustached lion dog." Another possible translation, depending upon interpretation, could be "barking hairy lion dog."

THE LHASA APSO'S RELATIONSHIP WITH OTHER BREEDS

The term "Apsok," or "Apso," is also used to describe the Tibetan Terrier, a longer-legged cousin of the Lhasa Apso. We are the ones, in the West, who have had the

The Tibetan Mastiff, shown here, was once kept in monasteries to protect from intruders.

The Tibetan Terrier, shown here with a pup, is the longer-legged cousin of the Lhasa Apso.

Opposite page: The Tibetan Terrier, shown here, bears quite a resemblance to his cousin, the Lhasa Apso.

temerity to add the word "Lhasa" to the breed's name, although clearly it was necessary to draw some distinction between the various Tibetan breeds. When these breeds first arrived in the West, there was great confusion among them.

In the distant past, it appears that the Lhasa Apso descended from European and Asiatic herding dogs, including the Hungarian Puli and Pumi. Certainly the breed has very close connections with two of the Tibetan breeds, the Tibetan Terrier and the Tibetan Spaniel, a close relation of which is the little-known Damchi of neighboring Bhutan. Another breed closely related to the Apso is the Shih Tzu; because of the similar outward appearance, the two breeds are frequently confused even today. However, the Shih Tzu was actually developed in China, although its roots go back to the Lhasa Apso of Tibet.

THE BREED'S INTRODUCTION TO BRITAIN

It has been erroneously quoted all too often that the Lhasa Apso first came to Britain in 1928, but it is essential to realize that the breed was there long before then. The first Lhasa Apso reported in Britain was in 1854, and certainly there were several representatives of the breed in Britain leading up the turn of the 20th century. There was, though, great confusion surrounding the naming of breeds at this time, and Lhasa Apsos and Tibetan Terriers founds themselves variously referred to as Thibetan, Kashmir, Bhuteer or Lhassa Terriers, and even as Thibet Poodles. In tracing back breed records, I have found differ-

TENZING AND THE APSO

Sherpa Tenzing Norgay, who climbed Mount Everest with Sir Edmund Hillary, owned Lhasa Apsos. He was given two by a Tibetan monk and took both with him to his home in Darjeeling, where he founded a kennel. Tenzing took a keen interest in the breed and enjoyed watching the breed on his visits to the UK.

The Shih Tzu has a close tie to its Tibetan cousin, the Lhasa. Today the two breeds are most distinct in size and construction.

exacerbates the problem to no end.

Because there were both Lhasa Apsos and Tibetan Terriers in Britain at that time, some were described as being as small as Maltese Terriers, but others as large as Russian Poodles. Clearly the discrepancies arose because there was, indeed, more than one breed. Something that all the dogs had in common was that their tails curled over their backs, a highly Tibetan characteristic of several different breeds known today.

ent puppies from individual litters registered under a number of different breed names, which

PRINCE HAJA

In 1933 it was reported that the Lhasa Apso Prince Haja of Tibet was actually bought as a mongrel for the sum of 15 shillings. He had been purchased from a monkey cage in Bedford. His owners had never heard of the breed but, having discovered what he was, registered the dog under his new name with The Kennel Club as "Pedigree and breeder unknown."

PRE-WORLD WAR I

There are some enchanting stories revolving around some of the earliest Apsos to leave Tibet. We hear of one that was carried on the saddle for miles and miles, with an attendant wreathed in turquoise. However, Apsos did not only belong to the very wealthy—one called Tuko was purchased from a market cart, the contents of which he was quite prepared to defend until grim death!

The Hon. Mrs. McLaren Morrison imported several foreign breeds to Britain. One of several Lhasa Apsos she owned was

Bhutan, renowned for begging at dog shows to raise money for the war fund. Even Princess Alexandra, a regular and enthusiastic visitor to shows, was known to have remarked that the little dog looked as if he was begging to leave the show. Sadly Bhutan contracted distemper and, said his owner, "…died at his post, so to speak."

INITIAL CHAMPIONSHIP STATUS

The breed known today as the Lhasa Apso gained championship status in Britain in 1908, although at this time it was shown in different classes for two different sizes, thus accommodating the Tibetan Terrier as well. One of the earliest champions of the breed,

The rare Pumi seems to be closely associated with the early development of the Lhasa Apso.

Eng. Ch. Rupso, was imported from Shigatse in 1907. When he died, his body was stuffed and preserved in the British Museum at Tring. To this day, Rupso is still labeled in the museum as a "Tibetan Terrier," although he was definitely a Lhasa Apso and measures slightly under 10 inches in height at withers.

BETWEEN WORLD WAR I AND WORLD WAR II

The war years took their toll on the breed and the Lhasa Apso was among several breeds that struggled to survive. In 1921 Colonel Bailey took over from Sir Charles Bell as Political Officer for Tibet, and Colonel Bailey and his wife brought back Apsos to Britain in 1928. This was the beginning of a traumatic time to follow, for soon after Shih Tzu were also imported to Britain from China and initially some thought them to be the same breed as the Lhasa Apso.

At first these dogs were shown together in the same classes, but differences were noted. The difference in length of forefaces was especially noted, leading to what was to become known as "the war of the noses." The ladies and gentlemen of the day who enthused about the breeds from Tibet and China engaged in heated, but polite, debate. The English Kennel Club also became involved. Finally the differences

The Puli is often thought of as being an early ancestor of the Apso. The Hungarian language derives from Mongolian, so perhaps there is proof of an ancient connection.

Opposite page: A glamorous Lhasa Apso, groomed American style.

were resolved and in 1934 breed standards were laid down for the Lhasa Apso, Tibetan Terrier, Tibetan Spaniel and Tibetan Mastiff. The Shih Tzu was classified as a separate breed and it was not represented by the newly formed Tibetan Breeds Association.

The breed had now finally arrived on a firm footing, but it did not compare with the popularity of the breed today. In 1935 only 12 Lhasa Apsos were entered at the famous Crufts dog show, which gives an indication of how little the breed was known in Britain at that time.

EFFECTS OF WORLD WAR II IN BRITAIN

There was severe curtailment of breeding programs during the World War II, and in Britain many people had their dogs destroyed. Thankfully, it was recognized that for lesser known breeds such drastic measures would spell disaster. Therefore, breeders of Lhasa Apsos were among those who were urged to make every effort to help their breeds survive

through those difficult times, provided that their dogs were not eating food that would deprive humans.

Between 1939 and 1944, only ten new puppies were registered in the breed, and late in the 1940s Miss Marjorie Wild's important Cotsvale strain was wiped out by hardpad and distemper. Thankfully the breed did manage to survive through some Ladkok- and Lamleh-bred dogs, these descending from the Baileys' imports from Tibet. It was clear, though, that bloodlines had dwindled and had once again to be built up. Just a handful of Lhasa Apsos, largely of unknown pedigree, was imported from Tibet before the Chinese banned all movement of dogs from the country.

THE 1950S
Numbers of Kennel Club registrations had risen gradually so that by 1956 it was felt that the breed was strong enough to break away from the Tibetan Breeds Association and form its own club. This saw the beginning of the Lhasa Apso Club, even though there were only 27 members at the club's first Annual General Meeting and fewer than half of them owned Apsos.

In 1959 the name of the breed was changed to Tibetan Apso, as it felt that this was the only breed from Tibet that did not bear the country's name. However, the change of name did not last long; by 1970 the name had once again reverted to Lhasa Apso.

CHAMPIONSHIP STATUS REGAINED
It was in May of 1964 that the English Kennel Club announced that Lhasa Apso registrations were sufficient in number for Challenge Certificate status to be restored. The first set of Challenge Certificates (CCs), required for a dog to become a champion in the UK, went on offer in 1965, a year in which nine sets were awarded. The first Apso to gain a post-war championship title, by dint of winning three CCs under different judges, was Brackenbury Gunga Din of Verles. Owned by Mrs. Daphne Hesketh Williams, Gunga Din won his third and crowning CC at the West of England Ladies Kennel Society (WELKS) under judge Miss Wild (Cotsvale), who had owned Lhasa Apsos since around the turn of the century.

WELCOME TO TIBET

The Lhasa Apso's homeland, Tibet, is a high table land; the plains around Lhasa are about 2 miles above sea level. In size Tibet is equal to France, Germany and Great Britain combined, and temperatures vary considerably. Within the space of a day, temperature may rise from below 32 to 100 degrees Farenheit.

A lovely Apso puppy is Modhish Mumbo Jumbo Millie at about one month of age. Her striking color pattern is evident even at a very young age.

The winner of the Bitch CC at that same show was Beryl Harding's Brackenbury Chigi-Gyemo, who was the first bitch in the breed to gain her crown, an accolade that came later that same year.

Since then the breed has gone on from strength to strength in Britain, and is one of the most popular breeds in the Utility Group, ranking in the top 20 most popular breeds of all in terms of Kennel Club registrations.

The breed has certainly hit high spots with Eng. Ch. Saxonsprings Hackensack winning Best in Show at Crufts in 1984, and Eng. Ch. Saxonsprings Fresno and Eng. Ch. Saxonsprings Tradition winning Top Dog All Breeds in 1982 and in 1998, respectively.

THE LHASA APSO IN THE US
An American by the name of Suydam Cutting was a world traveler, and after World War I went on an expedition to Tibet with a

brother of Theodore Roosevelt. Mr. Cutting went back to Tibet around 1930 when he met His Holiness the Dalai Lama, and subsequently sent him four dogs as a gift. As a result, a correspondence friendship developed between them and early in 1933, the first month of the Year of the Water Bird, HH the Dalai Lama sent to Mr. Cutting and his wife two Lhasa Apsos. Two more Apsos followed and then, in 1950, HH the 14th Dalai Lama sent another pair. These last two, Le and Phema, both became American champions. Sadly, Phema never had a litter, but Le sired several offspring.

The Cuttings' home was at Hamilton Farm in Gladstone, New Jersey, where the Apsos were supervised by Fred Huyler and James Anderson, who bred and showed Apsos under the Hamilton affix. Mr. Huyler was later to become the very first President of the American Lhasa Apso Club.

Although other people also played an important part in the Lhasa Apso's early history in the US, it was largely through the Cuttings and their Hamilton Kennels that the breed initially found its place on the American show scene. Their endeavors played an important role leading up to the American Kennel Club's recognition of the breed in 1935. The Cuttings were greatly interested in preserving the heritage of

the Lhasa Apso and, with the help of their associates, they achieved their goal. Selection of breeding stock was rigorous and the Hamilton dogs became famous worldwide for their uniformity of type.

The American breed standard was also drawn up in 1935, but, during the breed's early years in America, confusion raised its head in the breed once again. From 1937 some dogs were imported to the US, where they were registered in good faith as Lhasa Apsos. Unfortunately, they were actually Shih Tzu. Before their true identity was recognized, some of the dogs were bred from, but this practice was stopped in 1950. In consequence, many American Lhasa Apsos carry Shih Tzu blood in their pedigrees, although this does not apply to all, for some lines remained clear in those formative years.

To explain the breeding behind these imports is complex to say the least, but in their background were four of the Hutchins' and Brownriggs' Shih Tzu, Lung Fu Ssu, Tang, Hibou and Yangtze, who had been involved in the controversy between breeders in the early years in Britain.

In 1960 Mrs. Winifred Drake of the Drax kennels in Florida imported the dog, Ramblersholt Le Pon, and the bitch, Ramblersholt Shahnaz, from Mrs. Florence Dudman in England. The bitch became a champion and also won her American Lhasa Apso Club Register of Merit Award.

Another import to the US was Chumpa of Furzyhurst, who went to live in California with Mrs. Albertram McFadden of Lui Gi kennels. Not only did Chumpa become a champion but he also sired several champions himself. His grandson, Ch. Lui Gi's Shigat-zoo, went on to the San Saba kennel in Texas and later, in 1966, to the Cho Sen kennel in Kentucky.

Another of the early kennels in this breed that produced one of the bloodlines behind today's stock is Mrs. Dorothy Sabine de Gray's Las Sa Gre kennel in California. Mrs.

de Gray imported from England Ch. Fardale Fu Ssi, who was registered in the US as a Lhasa Apso but was, in fact, a Shih Tzu. She also owned a bitch called Las Sa Gre, who was of uncertain background. She might possibly also have been a Shih Tzu, though without any AKC background information this cannot be confirmed, and she might indeed have been an Apso. Whatever she was, over the years to come, Las Sa Gre's offspring, combined with Apsos from other lines, produced some very notable dogs in the breed's history in the US.

Another bloodline that came into America was from Chinese

A smartly coiffed Lhasa Apso is the product of dedicated breeding and proper care and rearing.

Apsos at home in the Himalayas. These dogs look much different than those in full show coat.

imports shortly before World War II. William Patch, a navy officer, bought littermates Ming Tai and Tai Ho from Mrs. Harvey Hall of Shanghai. While she was in quarantine in Hawaii, Tai Ho gave birth to three puppies, sired by her own father, Rags. Two other imports from China were Shanghai, of the same breeding as the first two, and Lhassa.

Early history of this breed in the US also goes back to dogs brought in from Canada in the early 1930s. The first two to come in from Canada here were the bitch, Dinkie, and the dog, Taikoo of Kokonor. Indeed the first two Lhasa Apsos registered after AKC recognition in 1935 were Tarzan of Kokonor and Empress of Kokonor, bred in 1933 by Miss Torrible and owned by Bruce Heathcote of Berkley, California.

When the Lhasa Apso was first classified in the AKC's group system, the breed (once called the Lhassa Terrier) was included in the Terrier Group, but this categorization changed in 1959, when it was transferred to the Non-Sporting Group, where it has remained.

In 1961, Mrs. Cutting died, and her husband sold the Hamilton Lhasa Apsos to Mrs. Dorothy Cohen of Karma kennels in Las Vegas. Mrs. Cohen is believed to have improved coat quality and texture in her breeding program, and also to have improved upon head and bite, though still retaining the merits of the Hamilton dogs. In September 1974 she announced that she would no longer be breeding Lhasa Apsos, and in doing so she published a list showing her 71 champions, many of which appear behind pedigrees today. Mrs. Cohen was a much-respected breeder, who passed away in 1977.

Numerous Lhasa Apsos and breeders have achieved high accolades. Records have been made and subsequently broken by others, but we cannot close this section without mentioning the wonderful win of Ch. Yojimbo Orion, who was the first Lhasa Apso to win his Group at the famous Westminster Show in 1977. Indeed the breed has gone on from strength to strength in America, and long may it continue to do so, with dogs having been exported all over the world, where many have made their mark.

AT HOME IN THE HIMALAYAS
Lhasa Apsos do, of course, still exist in their homeland and in the surrounding Himalayan regions, where they are still very much cherished. One can only hope that the breed in the Western World does not become so excessively glamorized that the Tibetans no longer recognize the stalwart little dog that has shared their lives for so very many generations.

THE LHASA APSO THROUGHOUT THE WORLD
The Lhasa Apso has made a significant impact on the dog-showing world in many countries, with many enthusiastic support-

In Tibet, all long-coated dogs are called "Apsok."

Lhasa Apsos are found worldwide in the homes of discerning dog lovers. It is easy to see why they are appreciated since they are beautiful, intelligent, loyal and obedient.

The internationally acclaimed Lhasa can be found throughout the world—ranging from the cold climate of Iceland to tropical Cuba.

ers in almost every corner of the globe. The author has been fortunate enough to judge the breed as far south as Australia and as far north as Scandinavia, finding high-quality specimens in both locations.

In countries where the Lhasa Apso is perhaps not so numerically strong, breeders' enthusiasm seems just as vibrant, for such a remarkable and endearing breed is sure to have admirers wherever it is found. There is now even one solitary Lhasa Apso in Iceland, where this lucky young lady feels very much at home in the snowy clime.

Lhasa Apsos are very family-oriented dogs. They want to live with and become part of their human families. This Apso is quite at home on his own comfortable blanket.

Characteristics of the
LHASA APSO

The Lhasa Apso is undoubtedly an entrancing and enchanting little breed, but his temperament, if typical, is not always easy to understand. In consequence, the Lhasa Apso is not an ideal pet for every home. Although of manageable size, to keep a Lhasa Apso in gloriously long, well-groomed coat takes a lot of work, so that, too, is an important consideration. Some owners of pet Apsos prefer to keep their dogs in short coat; this is perfectly acceptable, but is not suitable for the show ring. Of course, regular coat maintenance is still important, whether the coat is kept long or short.

During the last couple of decades, the Lhasa Apso has become highly popular, with thousands of Lhasa pups registered with the AKC each year. Although the breed has distinquished itself in the show ring, there is much more to an Apso than an elegant dog in full show coat, gliding around a big ring under the spotlights at a major dog show. A Lhasa Apso is a very special dog and needs a very special kind of owner, one who can understand a dog whose ancestors were raised in a tough environment on "The Roof of the World."

PHYSICAL CHARACTERISTICS

The Lhasa Apso is a fairly small breed, though not as small as some. It is sturdy for its size, with good muscle. The ideal height is 10 to 11 inches and in theory bitches should be a little smaller, and weight is usually between 15 and 19 lbs, although some are a little heavier.

The head of the breed is often much admired, but the heavy head furnishings somewhat conceal the lovely Tibetan expression. In the show ring the hair is always worn down, but at home the majority of owners tie up the hair in two bands, one on either side of the head. This helps to keep the face hair reasonably clean, avoids breakage of hair at

Even with the hair completely covering the face, the Lhasa Apso's long eyelashes serve to keep the hair out of the dog's eyes.

Opposite page: For the show ring, the Lhasa Apso's hair is always worn over the face, but at home most owners tie up the hair in two bands.

its ends and makes it easier for the dog to see. It is not always realized, though, that the eyelashes of a Lhasa Apso are very long, so the hair does not actually fall into the eyes. Obviously in the breed's homeland the hair was never tied up; instead, the fall acted as protection against the strong sunlight and whiteness of the snowy terrain.

Because so many novices confuse the Lhasa Apso with the Shih Tzu, it is necessary to explain that the head shape of the two breeds is quite different. The skull of the Apso is much narrower than that of the Shih Tzu and the Apso's eye is less round, thus not as prominent. The Shih Tzu's nose, too, is shorter than that of the Apso, which measures about 1.5 inches. There are also differences in body. The rib cage of the Shih Tzu is more barreled than that of the Apso, and the Shih Tzu is somewhat lower slung.

Unfortunately, the beauty of the Lhasa Apso's coat is sometimes taken to extremes and many owners, out of fear that the dogs will damage their coats, do not allow their dogs the free exercise needed to build up muscle naturally. Provided that an Apso's coat is of typically hard texture and that the coat is cared for regularly, a coat can still retain its glory even when the dog is allowed to exercise freely. Some owners of show Apsos do not allow their dogs to do much more than to spend virtually their whole lives inside crates. These owners may indeed end up with dogs whose coats look good in the show ring, but they do not end up with happy, healthy dogs!

Coat condition is essential to success in the show ring. Some owners do not even let their Apsos outside, except for outdoor shows, for fear of the dogs' soiling or damaging their coats.

Although this can be done at home, many owners find it easier to have the coat professionally trimmed about three times each year. Attention to the coat is, of course, also necessary between trims.

The Lhasa Apso can be found in a wide variety of colors, including golden, sandy, honey, dark grizzle, smoke, parti-color, black, white and brown. All colors are equally acceptable, and there are many unusual color combinations that crop up. A parti-colored dog is one in which the coat is made up of two distinct colors, one of which is white. Thus one finds gold-and-white, black-and-white, gray-and-white or sable-and-white parti-colors, all of which are equally acceptable.

Although liver- and chocolate-colored Lhasa Apsos are produced from time to time, these are not favored in the show ring. This is because their nose pigmentation is of corresponding color to the coat, and the standard states that the nose is to be black.

Lhasa Apsos can be kept in a short coat or a long coat, but only Apsos with full coats can be shown in conformation.

COLORS AND COAT

A Lhasa Apso in full show coat is a magnificent sight, but to keep a coat in this condition certainly involves time and dedication. The Lhasa Apso has not only a long flowing top coat but also a good undercoat. This means that merely grooming the top layer may initially give a reasonably good overall appearance, but in no time at all the undercoat will start to form knots. Knots and tangles are incredibly difficult to remove if allowed to build up, so this aspect of coat care must be taken seriously into consideration before setting your heart on the breed.

Many Lhasa Apso pets are, however, kept in short coat, known usually as "pet trim."

Lhasa Apsos occur in many colors. The honey-colored dog, shown here, is a prime example of a show-quality Lhasa Apso.

Because there is no color preference in Lhasa Apsos, in truth an owner should not be swayed by color. Having said that, it is only natural that some people have a purely personal preference, just as they might for the color of their own clothing or furniture. What really matters are the dog's construction, temperament, general health and coat quality. However, if choosing a pet, color may indeed be a deciding factor, and this is entirely understandable. After all, there is no point in buying a gray Lhasa Apso and, love the dog as you might, thinking for the next 14 years or so that it was a pity you didn't have the golden color you really preferred!

TAIL
The tail of the Lhasa Apso should be high set and carried well over the back. Occasionally, if you feel carefully, you may find a small kink at the end of the tail. This is perfectly normal, and you must certainly never endeavor to straighten it out as this would cause injury. This is an old characteristic of the breed

The mystical look of a well-groomed Lhasa Apso. It is evident why these dogs were often compared to lions in Tibetan mythology. Inset: Yes, there are eyes hiding under all that hair!

that, sadly, now seems to be dying out.

As with the rest of the dog, the tail coat will need regular attention—it, too, is long and flowing. However, because of the breed's size, the Apso's tail is unlikely to knock your precious vases onto the floor, as might the enthusiastic tail of a larger dog such as a Dalmatian or Labrador Retriever. The tail of a Lhasa Apso is never docked.

PERSONALITY

The breed standard describes the Lhasa Apso as being gay and assertive, but somewhat chary with strangers. Whether chary or aloof, a typical Lhasa Apso will not be overly friendly with strangers, but prefers to take a more reserved stance. An Apso will usually bark as someone approaches the house, then, when the visitor has been welcomed and accepted by the owner, the dog will take a seat at a little distance. From his chosen vantage point, the dog will always be able to view what is going on around him, but will only become involved in activities if he so chooses.

Often it takes an Apso some time to make friends but, once he has decided to do so, the friendship he offers is sincere. It is always best to allow an Apso to approach any visitor to the home

The Lhasa Apso is an alert, steady dog that takes some time to warm up to strangers.

in his own good time; this makes for a much happier eventual relationship.

With family and owners, an Apso is very devoted, but not all enjoy a cuddle as much as some owners would like. I have owned many Apsos over the years and have found their personalities each to be individual. Some certainly like more affection than others, and this applies to both dogs and bitches.

Apsos can be trained to obedience, but they do have a rather stubborn streak and do not always respond to your commands as rapidly as one might hope. There is no doubt in my own mind that Apsos like to think things out and

that when they do something it has to be because they want to—at least they have to give you that impression!

The Lhasa Apso does give a warning bark, for you will recall that this is what was expected of the breed in the monasteries of Tibet. However, it is not a particu-

TO DEW OR NOT TO DEW

Although there is no stipulation as to whether or not dewclaws should be removed on the Lhasa Apso, many breeders do like to have them removed when puppies are three days old. This makes nails easier to manage under the long adult coat.

larly high-pitched, piercing bark, and an Apso will usually stop barking quite quickly when he believes the situation is under control.

Although many Apsos get along well with other dogs, there are those who don't. This can depend very largely on upbringing and environment, and gender often has a large part to play in who gets along with whom. Undoubtedly there are some breeders who seem to have absolutely no problem in keeping several males and several females together in one group. However, in my own experience there have been limitations, and I know my experiences are shared by many.

Usually bitches will get along well with other females, but they tend to have disagreements around the times of their seasons. Usually this is easily controlled by sensible management, but some bitches can have very nasty disagreements, so one should always be on the lookout for trou-

PUFFS

The "puffs" is not a major problem, but it can be alarming and should always be investigated by the owner. There can be other reasons for such puffing; for example, a grass seed could be lodged in the dog's nasal cavity and would require immediate removal.

seem to mellow with maturity and lose any animosity they may have felt as youngsters.

HEALTH CONSIDERATIONS

Although not usually a serious problem, something that can frighten a new owner is the "puffs." This is a fairly frequent occurrence in the brachycephalic (short-nosed) breeds. Because of elongation of the soft palate, a dog will suddenly draw in short, sharp breaths and look very tense, usually standing four square as he does so. This is usually brought

ble that may be brewing. Personally, although I have often tried to keep two male Apsos together, I have never succeeded beyond puppyhood, for a problem always has ensued. Having said that, I have happily kept one male Apso (not used at stud) with two male Afghan Hounds and the three remained firm friends throughout their lives.

Dogs and bitches usually live together as great friends, but in my own experience I have only successfully kept one male with any number of bitches. Interestingly, I have found that bitches who do not get along together particularly well in their youth

CLIMB EV'RY MOUNTAIN

Some Lhasa Apsos are extremely great climbers—some can even scale a 6-foot fence. Thankfully most do not climb at all, but, since some are particularly adept, owners must always be aware of this possibility. Much to the surprise of their owners, some do not decide they will take to climbing until they are well into maturity!

Lhasa Apsos are hardy dogs but they do, occasionally, inherit or suffer from eye problems.

on by the dog's becoming very excited, but generally only lasts a matter of seconds. A quick and simple solution is to place your fingers over the dog's nostrils, thereby causing him to breathe only through his mouth.

The Lhasa Apso is, in general, a hardy little dog and usually a fairly healthy one, although there are a few veterinary and possibly hereditary problems that a new owner should be aware of. The only inherited problem officially recognized in the breed is progressive retinal atrophy (PRA). This is an eye disorder, not usually discovered until adulthood, from which a dog progressively goes blind. Often this is noticed first by night blindness, but total blindness is unfortunately the inevitable end result. Thankfully, there is no pain associated with this condition.

PRA has been discovered only recently in the Lhasa Apso and DNA testing is a goal toward which breeds are working, though this may still be a long way off. Currently, it is essential that both the sire and dam of a litter have their eyes tested prior to mating, and breeders have to use carefully their knowledge of hereditary factors in order to avoid, if possible, doubling up on the gene that carries this inherited disease.

Some Lhasa Apsos can suffer from "dry eye," something that seems to occur late in life. This can usually be managed with a combination of drugs designed to create artificial tears.

Some Lhasa Apsos are also found to have enlarged harderian glands; this condition is, more specifically, an enlargement of the nictitating membrane in the inner corner of the eye. This is commonly known as "cherry eye" and is easily noticed as a red swelling. This usually occurs

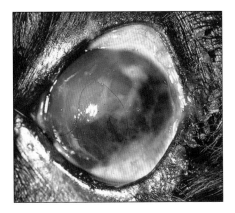

during puppyhood, sometimes in pups as young as about eight weeks of age. There are two methods of dealing with this problem. Currently "tucking" is the method most commonly used, but it used to be normal just to remove the gland so that the problem could not recur. However, it now appears that when the gland has been removed, the occurrence of "dry eye" later in life becomes more likely.

Because the Lhasa Apso is a breed that is relatively long-backed and low to the ground, one should always be on the alert for possible back problems, especially in a dog's later years. In an ideal world, Apsos should not be allowed to jump off furniture, but this is more easily said than done! At any sign of spinal injury, a vet should be contacted without delay; in some cases even complete recovery can be achieved. Unfortunately often partial paralysis results, but an affected dog can be fitted with a little wheeled cart to support his hind legs if the owner so desires. Obviously, caring for a dog who has suffered spinal injuries involves making serious decisions. All of the options, however distressful, must be discussed openly with your family and vet.

Keratoconjunctivit is sicca, or "dry eye," seen here in the right eye of a middle-aged dog, causes a characteristic thick mucus discharge as well as secondary corneal changes.

Due to the Lhasa's long-backed construction, injuries to the back and other problems are a concern for breeders and owners alike.

Physical Structure of the Lhasa Apso

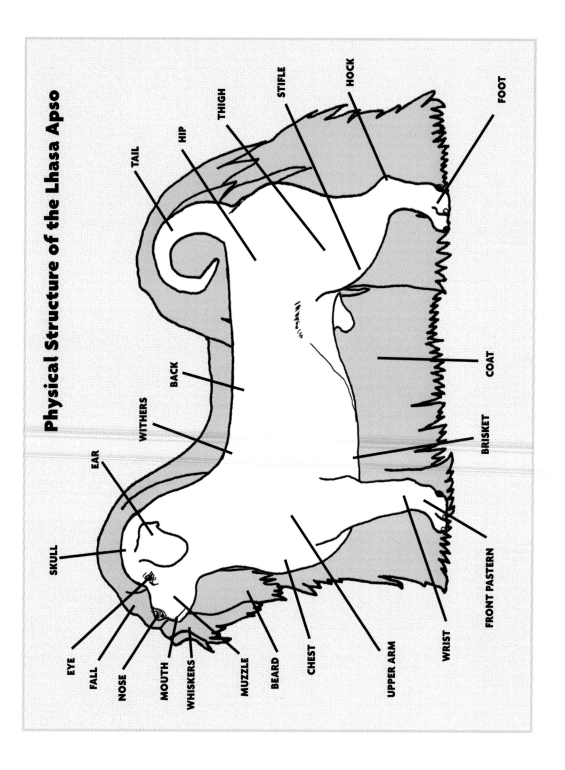

Breed Standard for the
LHASA APSO

The breed standard for the Lhasa Apso is effectively a "blueprint" for the breed. It sets down the various points of the dog in words, enabling a picture to be conjured up in the mind of the reader. However, this is more easily said than done. Not only do standards vary from country to country, but people's interpretations of breed standards vary also. It is this difference of interpretation that makes judges select different dogs for top honors, for

Quality in a Lhasa Apso shimmers through on the dog's coat, but what is under his magnificent coat is of equal or greater importance. Judges look for Lhasa Apsos with sound construction and overall balance.

their opinions differ as to which dog most closely fits the breed standard. That is not to say that a good dog does not win regularly under different judges, nor that an inferior dog may rarely even be placed at a show, at least not among quality competition.

The breed standard and presentation vary from the US to the UK, the author's homeland. The breed standard given here is that authorized by the American Kennel Club (AKC), in which the size clause is more flexible than that used in Britain, where the ideal height for dogs is 10 inches at shoulder, with bitches slightly smaller. Another significant differ-

ence is in the section on mouth and muzzle, for in Britain the standard only calls for a reverse scissor bite, the option of a level bite having been deleted from the standard many years ago. However, in the US, the bite may be level or slightly undershot.

It is true that for the show ring, most of the undercoat is groomed out for purposes of presentation, but we must never lose sight of the fact that the Lhasa Apso comes from a land with extremes of climate where a good undercoat is imperative for survival.

Now to the thorny question of dark tips, which in the US

The author is most passionate about the importance of dark ear tips on the Lhasa. This duo well illustrates this special breed hallmark.

may or may not be present on the ears and beard. Although not evident to non-breeders, this is related to the black nose pigment required in the standard. Breeding together, over a prolonged period of time, Apsos that carry no black coat pigment at all eventually lose depth of skin pigment. This can be seen especially on the nose, which loses color, not just in the winter months when "winter nose" can all too often be used as an excuse for poor pigmentation.

THE AMERICAN KENNEL CLUB STANDARD FOR THE LHASA APSO

Character: Gay and assertive, but chary of strangers.

Size: Variable, but about 10 inches or 11 inches at shoulder for dogs, bitches slightly smaller.

Color: All colors equally acceptable with or without dark tips to ears and beard.

Body Shape: The length from point of shoulders to point of buttocks longer than height at withers, well ribbed up, strong loin, well-developed quarters and thighs.

Coat: Heavy, straight, hard, not woolly nor silky, of good length, and very dense.

In profile, showing proper balance, structure and type, with a correct, mature coat.

Head study, showing proper structure and expression, groomed properly for the show ring.

Mouth and Muzzle: The preferred bite is either level or slightly undershot. Muzzle of medium length; a square muzzle is objectionable.

Head study, showing a dog with the coat divided into a topknot typical for the breed to show the eyes.

Head: Heavy head furnishings with good fall over eyes, good whiskers and beard; skull narrow, falling away behind the eyes in a marked degree, not quite flat, but not domed or apple-shaped; straight foreface of fair length. Nose black, the length from tip of nose to eye to be roughly about one-third of the total length from nose to back of skull.

Eyes: Dark brown, neither very large and full, nor very small and sunk.

A pet trim that is easily maintained and approximates a puppy's tousled appearance appeals to many people.

Ears: Pendant, heavily feathered.

Legs: Forelegs straight; both forelegs and hind legs heavily furnished with hair.

Feet: Well feathered, should be round and catlike, with good pads.

Tail and Carriage: Well feathered, should be carried well over back in a screw; there may be a kink at the end. A low carriage of stern is a serious fault.

While the Lhasa Apso's breed standard is concise but fairly self-explanatory, readers interested in showing their Apsos should learn as much as possible from established breeders and exhibitors. It is sensible to attend judges' seminars, often hosted by breed clubs. Here the finer points of the breed can be explained fully and discussed.

There are, however, a few further points that benefit from further elaboration in this book. Those not familiar with the Lhasa Apso often find it difficult to understand the construction of the mouth and most usual placement of teeth, which is "slightly undershot," or in British parlance, "reverse scissor." Often a new pet owner can be thoroughly dismayed when, taking his new puppy along to the vet for the first time, he is wrongly told that the mouth is incorrect.

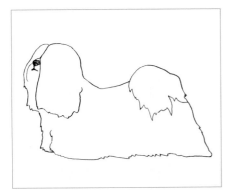

When evaluating coated breeds like the Lhasa Apso, the judge's or breeder's hands must discover what the sins the coat disguises; movement will reveal faults of structure and topline. (Left) Long backed, steep shoulders, high in rear. (Right) Too high on leg, short neck, low-set tail.

Level bites, in which the incisors meet edge to edge, are still found in the breed and in the US are considered correct, but a slightly undershot bite means that the upper teeth close just inside the lower. This is a highly functional bite. However, the lower teeth should not be too far forward of the upper set, nor should they be set into the jaw such that they protrude at a severe angle, for these not only look untypical but also are not at all a practical set of teeth. Normal scissors bites are also found, but these causes the typical Oriental expression to be lost. Another anomaly is the "parrot mouth," which is severely overshot. Thankfully this is a rare occurrence and is highly undesirable, so any puppies born with such a mouth should never be bred from.

Something not mentioned in the standard is the chin. However, all dedicated Apso breeders will agree that an Apso does need to have some chin to give the desired Oriental expression to which I have previously referred. Most dogs with slightly undershot

(Left) Soft topline, head and neck set forward, suggesting upright shoulders, and not much behind the tail, suggesting poor angulation behind. (Right) Short neck, loaded shoulders and wide front, poor tail set, weak topline, steep in the croup, which often accompanies a poor tail set.

bites do have sufficient chin, although there are exceptions.

Looking at the head of the Lhasa Apso in profile, the proportion from tip of nose to stop versus stop to back of skull should be 1 to 2. Thus, this is actually a partial-brachycephalic breed (partially short-nosed).

Length is measured from "point of shoulders to point of buttocks." This is the foremost

Champion-quality dogs and bitches are used for breeding in order to perpetuate the best qualities of the Lhasa Apso.

point of the shoulder blade, not
the top tip of the blade as has
sometimes been misreported.
Thus, in effect, the Apso is really
not much longer than the majority
of breeds of dog. It should
certainly not be so long that it
resembles a train!

In the AKC breed standard,
there is no mention of the movement or gait of the Lhasa Apso, but
in Britain it is described as "Free

and jaunty." An incorrect action
found in the hind movement of
many Apsos today is that the dog
shows the full pad of the hind feet
as he moves away. This is the
correct movement for a Shih Tzu,
but certainly not for a Lhasa Apso.
When an Apso moves away, you
should only be able to see a third
of the pad, for the feet should not
be kicked up so high into the air
that the whole foot is visible.

LHASA APSO

You probably decided on a Lhasa Apso as your choice of pet following a visit to the home of a friend or acquaintance, where you saw a well-behaved Apso wandering happily around the house, politely minding his own business. However, as a new owner, you must realize that a good deal of care, commitment and careful training goes into raising a boisterous puppy in order for that pup to turn into a well-adjusted adult.

In deciding to take on a new puppy, you will be committing yourself to around 14 years of responsibility, possibly longer. No dog should be discarded after a few months, or even a few years, after the novelty has worn off. Instead, your Lhasa Apso should be joining your household to spend the rest of his days with you.

Temperamentally, a Lhasa Apso can be more difficult to look after than many other breeds, so you will need to carry out a certain amount of training. However, unlike some of the larger breeds, the Apso will not respond well to overly strict training. Instead, you will need to take a firm but gentle approach in order to get the very best out of your pet.

A Lhasa Apso generally likes to be clean around the house, but you will need to teach your puppy what is and is not expected. You will need to be consistent in your instructions; it is no good accepting certain behavior one day and not the next. Not only will your puppy simply not understand, he will be utterly confused. Your Lhasa Apso will want to please you, so you will need to demonstrate clearly how he should go about doing this.

Although the dog you are taking into your home will be fairly small, and in this regard less troublesome than a large dog, there will undoubtedly be a period of settling in. This will be great fun, but you must be prepared for mishaps around the home during the first few weeks of your lives together. It will be important that breakables are kept well out of harm's way, and you will have to think twice about where you place hot cups of coffee or anything breakable. Accidents can and do happen, so you will need to think ahead so as to avoid these. Electric cables must be carefully concealed, and your puppy must be taught what he can and cannot touch.

Before making your commitment to a new puppy, do also think carefully about your future vacation plans>. Depending on where you wish to travel, your dog may or may not be able to go with you. If you have thought things through carefully and discussed the matter thoroughly with all of the members of your family, hopefully you will have come to the right decision. If you decide that a Lhasa Apso should join your family, this will hopefully be a happy long-term relationship for all parties concerned.

BUYING A LHASA APSO PUPPY
Although you may be looking for a Lhasa Apso as a pet, rather than as a show dog, this does not mean that you want a dog that is in any way "second-rate." A caring breeder will have brought up the entire litter of puppies with the same amount of dedication, and a puppy destined for a pet home should be just as healthy as one that hopes to end up in the show ring.

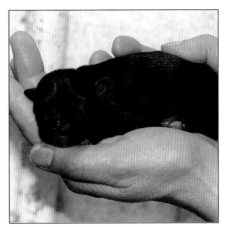

A tiny puppy is a huge responsibility. A breeder puts in a lot of energy to raise pups from day one and wants to ensure that his pups only go to the best homes.

ARE YOU PREPARED?

Unfortunately, when a puppy is bought by someone who does not take into consideration the time and attention that dog ownership requires, it is the puppy who suffers when he is either abandoned or placed in a shelter by a frustrated owner. So all of the "homework" you do in preparation for your pup's arrival will benefit you both. The more informed you are, the more you will know what to expect and the better equipped you will be to handle the ups and downs of raising a puppy. Hopefully, everyone in the household is willing to do his part in raising and caring for the pup. The anticipation of owning a dog often brings a lot of promises from excited family members: "I will walk him every day," "I will feed him," "I will housetrain him," etc., but these things take time and effort, and promises can easily be forgotten once the novelty of the new pet has worn off.

TEMPERAMENT COUNTS

Your selection of a good puppy can be determined by your needs. A show potential or a good pet? It is your choice. Every puppy, however, should be of good temperament. Although show-quality puppies are bred and raised with emphasis on physical conformation, responsible breeders strive for equally good temperament. Do not buy from a breeder who concentrates solely on physical beauty at the expense of personality.

Because you have carefully selected this breed, you will want a Lhasa Apso that is a typical specimen, both in looks and in temperament. In your endeavors to find such a puppy, you will have to select the breeder with care. The American Kennel Club and the American Lhasa Apso Club will almost certainly be able to give you names of contacts within local Lhasa Apso breed clubs. These people can possibly put you in touch with breeders who may have puppies for sale. However, although they can point you in the right direction, it will be up to you to do your homework carefully.

Even though you are probably not looking for a show dog, it is always a good idea to visit a show so that you can see quality specimens of the breed. This will also give you an opportunity to meet breeders who will probably be able to answer some of your queries. In addition, you will get some idea about which breeders appear to take the best care of their stock and which are likely to have given their puppies the best possible start in life. Something else you may be able to decide upon is which color appeals to you most, although this is purely personal preference.

When buying your puppy, you will need to know about vaccinations, both those already given and those still due. It is important that any injections already given by a verterinarian are documented in writing. A worming routine is also vital for any young puppy, so the breeder should be able to tell you exactly what treatment has been given, when it was administered and how you should continue.

Clearly, when selecting a puppy, the one you choose must be in good condition. The coat should look healthy and there should be no discharge from the eyes or nose. Ears should also be clean, and of course there should be absolutely no sign of parasites. The pup's skin should be clean and healthy-looking, with no indication of a rash. Of course, the puppy you choose should not have evidence of loose or otherwise irregular bowel movements.

As in several other breeds, some Lhasa Apso puppies have umbilical hernias. An umbilical hernia can be a seen as a small lump on the tummy where the

PUPPY APPEARANCE

Your puppy should have a well-fed appearance but not a distended abdomen, which may indicate worms or incorrect feeding, or both. The body should be firm, with a solid feel. The skin of the abdomen should be pale pink and clean, without signs of scratching or rash. Check the hind legs to see if the breeder has had the dewclaws removed.

umbilical cord was attached. It is preferable not to have such a hernia on any puppy, so you should check for this at the outset. If a hernia is present, you should discuss the severity of the problem with the breeder. Most umbilical hernias are safe, but your vet should keep an eye on it in case surgery is needed.

Finally, a few words of advice: find out as much about your prospective pup's background as you can. Don't be afraid to ask questions of the breeder. Always request that you see the puppy's dam and, if possible, the sire. While frequently the sire will not be owned by the breeder of the litter, a photograph may be available for you to see. Ask if the breeder has any other of the puppy's relations that you could meet. For example, there may be an older half-sister or brother, and it would be interesting for you to see how this dog has turned out— eventual size, coat quality, temperament and so on.

Be sure, too, that if you decide to buy a puppy, all relevant documentation is provided at the time of sale. You will need a copy of

PEDIGREE VS. REGISTRATION CERTIFICATE

Too often new owners are confused between these two important documents. Your puppy's pedigree, essentially a family tree, is a written record of a dog's genealogy of three generations or more. The pedigree will show you the names as well as performance titles of all the dogs in your pup's background. Your breeder must provide you with a registration application, with his part properly filled out. You must complete the application and send it to the AKC with the proper fee. The seller must provide you with complete records to identify the puppy. The AKC requires that the seller provide the buyer with the following: breed; sex, color and markings; date of birth; litter number (when available); names and registration numbers of the parents; breeder's name; and date sold or delivered.

the pedigree, and ideally registration papers, vaccination certificates and a feeding chart so that you know exactly how the puppy has been fed and how you should continue. Some careful breeders provide their puppy buyers with a small amount of food. This prevents the risk of an upset tummy, allowing for a gradual change of diet if that particular brand of food is not locally available.

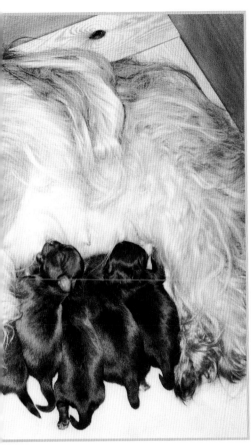

done your research and found a responsible, conscientious person who breeds quality Lhasa Apsos and who should be a reliable source of help as you and your puppy adjust to life together. If you have observed a litter in action, you have obtained a first-hand look at the dynamics of a puppy "pack" and, thus, you have learned about each pup's individual personality—perhaps you have even found one that particularly appeals to you.

However, even if you have not yet found the Lhasa Apso puppy of your dreams, observing pups will help you learn to recognize certain behavior and to determine what a pup's behavior indicates about his temperament. You will be able to pick out which pups are the leaders, which ones are less outgoing, which ones are confident, which ones are shy, playful, friendly, aggressive, etc.

Pups should stay with their dam until they are at least 12 weeks old. Breeders will not allow the puppies to leave their dam until they have been weaned and properly socialized and reared.

COMMITMENT OF OWNERSHIP

After considering all of these factors, you have most likely already made some very important decisions about selecting your puppy. You have chosen the Lhasa Apso, which means that you have decided which characteristics you want in a dog and what type of dog will best fit into your family and lifestyle. If you have selected a breeder, you have gone a step further—you have

TIME TO GO HOME

Breeders rarely release puppies until they are eight to ten weeks of age. This is an acceptable age for most breeds of dog, excepting small breeds, which are not released until around 12 weeks. If a breeder has a puppy that is 12 weeks of age or older, it is likely well socialized and house-trained.

Litter brother (left) and litter sister (right). Even at this young age, you can clearly differentiate between dog and bitch.

Equally as important, you will learn to recognize what a healthy pup should look and act like. All of these things will help you in your search, and when you find the Lhasa Apso that was meant for you, you will know it!

Researching your breed, selecting a responsible breeder and observing as many pups as possible are all important steps on the way to dog ownership. It may seem like a lot of effort...and you have not even brought the pup home yet! Remember, though, you cannot be too careful when it comes to deciding on the type of dog you want and finding out about your prospective pup's background. Buying a puppy is not—or *should* not be—just another whimsical purchase. This is one instance in which you actually do get to choose your own family! You may be thinking that buying a puppy should be fun—it should not be so serious and so much work. Keep in mind that your puppy is not a cuddly stuffed toy or deco-

ARE YOU A FIT OWNER?

If the breeder from whom you are buying a puppy asks you a lot of personal questions, do not be insulted. Such a breeder wants to be sure that you will be a fit provider for his puppy.

rative lawn ornament, but a creature that will become a real member of your family. You will come to realize that, while buying a puppy is a pleasurable and exciting endeavor, it is not something to be taken lightly. Relax…the fun will start when the pup comes home!

Always keep in mind that a puppy is nothing more than a baby in a furry disguise…a baby who is virtually helpless in a human world and who trusts his owner for fulfillment of his basic needs for survival. In addition to food, water and shelter, your pup needs care, protection, guidance and love. If you are not prepared to commit to this, then you are not prepared to own a dog.

"Wait a minute," you say. "How hard could this be? All of my neighbors own dogs and they seem to be doing just fine. Why should I have to worry about all of this?" Well, you should not worry about it; in fact, you will probably find that once your Lhasa Apso pup gets used to his new home, he will fall into his place in the family quite naturally. But it never hurts to emphasize the commitment of dog ownership. With some time and patience, it is really not too difficult to raise a curious and exuberant Lhasa Apso pup to become a well-adjusted and well-mannered adult dog—a dog that could be your most loyal friend.

A proud mother with her newborn litter. Note the guard rail inside the whelping box to prevent the bitch from accidentally suffocating a pup.

PREPARING PUPPY'S PLACE IN YOUR HOME

Researching your breed and finding a breeder are only two aspects of the "homework" you will have to do before bringing your Lhasa Apso puppy home. You will also have to prepare your home and family for the new addition. Much as you would prepare a nursery for a newborn baby, you will need to designate a place in your home that will be the puppy's own.

YOUR SCHEDULE . . .

If you lead an erratic, unpredictable life, with daily or weekly changes in your work requirements, consider the problems of owning a puppy. The new puppy has to be fed regularly, socialized (loved, petted, handled, introduced to other people) and, most importantly, allowed to go outdoors for house-training. As the dog gets older, he can be more tolerant of deviations in his feeding and relief schedule.

How you prepare your home will depend on how much freedom the dog will be allowed. Will he be confined to one room or a specific area in the house, or will he be allowed to roam as he pleases? Whatever you decide, you must ensure that he has a place that he can "call his own."

When you bring your new puppy into your home, you are bringing him into what will become his home as well. Obviously, you did not buy a puppy so that he could take over your house, but in order for a puppy to grow into a stable, well-adjusted dog, he has to feel comfortable in his surroundings. Remember, he is leaving the warmth and security of his mother and littermates, as well as the familiarity of the only place he has ever known, so it is important to make his transition as easy as possible. By preparing a place in your home for the puppy, you are making him feel as welcome as

QUALITY FOOD

The cost of food must be mentioned. All dogs need a good-quality food with an adequate supply of protein to develop their bones and muscles properly. Most dogs are not picky eaters but, unless fed properly, can quickly succumb to skin problems.

possible in a strange new place. It should not take him long to get used to it, but the sudden shock of being transplanted is somewhat traumatic for a young pup. Imagine how a small child would feel in the same situation—that is how your puppy must be feeling. It is up to you to reassure him and to let him know, "Little Apso, you are going to like it here!"

WHAT YOU SHOULD BUY

CRATE
To someone unfamiliar with the use of crates in dog training, it may seem like punishment to shut a dog in a crate, but this is not the case at all. Crates are not cruel—crates have many humane and highly effective uses in dog care and training. For example, crate training is a very popular and the most successful housebreaking method used by trainers today. A crate can keep your dog safe during travel; and, perhaps most importantly, a crate provides your dog with a safe place of his own in your home. It serves as a "doggie bedroom" of sorts—your Lhasa Apso can curl up in his crate when he wants to sleep or when he just needs a break. Many dogs sleep in their

The wire crate has the advantages of being easier to clean and allowing the dog more contact with the people around him.

Your local pet shop probably has a fine array of crates. Buy a crate that will be suitable for a Lhasa Apso both as a puppy and when fully grown.

A young Lhasa begins his training. Learning to stand like a champion is an essential lesson for the aspiring show pup.

PHOTO COURTESY OF DOSKOCIL

and disadvantages to each type. For example, a wire crate is more open, allowing the air to flow through and affording the dog a view of what is going on around him, while a fiberglass crate is sturdier. Both can double as car-travel crates, providing protection for the dog. The size of the crate is another thing to consider. Puppies do not stay puppies forever, but Lhasa Apsos do not increase too greatly in size so you should easily be able to select a medium-sized crate that will serve into adulthood.

crates overnight. When lined with a soft crate pad, with a favorite toy inside, a crate becomes a cozy pseudo-den for your dog. Like his ancestors, he too will seek out the comfort and retreat of a den—you just happen to be providing him with a safe, clean place to call his own.

As far as purchasing a crate, the type that you buy is up to you. It will most likely be one of the two most popular types: wire or fiberglass. There are advantages

BEDDING

A crate pad in the dog's crate will help the dog feel more at home and you may also give him a small blanket. These things will take the place of the leaves, twigs, etc., that the pup would use in the wild to make a den; the pup can make his own "burrow" in the crate. Although your pup is far removed from his den-making ancestors, the denning instinct is still a part of his genetic makeup. Secondly, until you bring your pup home, he has been sleeping amid the warmth of his dam and littermates, and while a blanket is not the same as a warm, breathing body, it still provides heat and something with which to snuggle. You will want to wash your pup's bedding frequently in case he has an accident in his crate, and replace or remove any pad or blanket that becomes ragged and starts to fall apart.

TOYS

Toys are a must for dogs of all ages, especially for curious playful pups. Puppies

CRATE-TRAINING TIPS

During crate training, you should partition off the section of the crate in which the pup stays. If he is given too big an area, this will hinder your training efforts. Crate training is based on the fact that a dog does not like to soil his sleeping quarters, so it is ineffective to keep a pup in an area that is so big that he can eliminate in one end and get far enough away from it to sleep. Also, you want to make the crate den-like for the pup. Blankets and a favorite toy will make the crate cozy for the small pup; as he grows, you may want to evict some of his "roommates" to make more room. It will take some coaxing at first, but be patient. Given some time to get used to it, your pup will adapt to his new home-within-a-home quite nicely.

Your Lhasa will enjoy the opportunity to explore his new home indoors and out, under your supervision and with his safety first and foremost in your mind.

into"—everything tastes great!

Lhasa Apso puppies are fairly devoted chewers, so only the safest toys should be offered to them. Breeders advise owners to resist stuffed toys, because they can become de-stuffed in no time. The overly excited pup may ingest the stuffing, which is neither digestible nor nutritious.

Similarly, squeaky toys are quite popular, but must be avoided for the Lhasa Apso. Perhaps a squeaky toy can be used as an aid in training, but not for free play. If a pup "disembowels" one of these, the small plastic squeaker inside can be dangerous if swallowed. Monitor the condition of all your pup's toys carefully and get rid of any that have been chewed to the point of becoming potentially dangerous.

Be careful of natural bones, which have a tendency to splinter into sharp, dangerous pieces. Also be careful of rawhide, which can turn into pieces that are easy to swallow or into a mushy mess on your carpet.

are the "children" of the dog world, and what child does not love toys? Chew toys provide enjoyment to both dog and owner—your dog will enjoy playing with his favorite toys, while you will enjoy the fact that they distract him from your expensive shoes and leather sofa. Puppies love to chew; in fact, chewing is a physical need for pups as they are teething, and everything looks appetizing! The full range of your possessions—from old dishcloth to Oriental rug—are fair game in the eyes of a teething pup. Puppies are not all that discerning when it comes to finding something to literally "sink their teeth

LEAD

A nylon lead is probably the best option as it is the most resistant to puppy teeth should your pup take a liking to chewing on his lead. Of course, this is a habit that should be nipped in the bud, but, if your pup likes to chew on his lead, he has a very slim chance of being able to chew through the strong nylon. Nylon leads are also lightweight, which is good for a young Lhasa Apso who is just getting used to the idea of walking on a lead. For everyday walking and safety purposes, the nylon lead is a good choice. As your pup grows up and gets used to walking on the lead, you may want to purchase a flexible lead. These leads allow you to extend the length to give the dog a broader area to explore or to shorten the length to keep the dog close to you. Of course there are special leads for training and showing purposes; these are made of nylon but are too flimsy for daily walks.

TOYS, TOYS, TOYS!

With a big variety of dog toys available, and so many that look like they would be a lot of fun for a dog, be careful in your selection. It is amazing what a set of puppy teeth can do to an innocent-looking toy; so, obviously, safety is a major consideration. Be sure to choose the most durable products that you can find. Hard nylon bones and toys are a safe bet, and many of them are offered in different scents and flavors that will be sure to capture your dog's attention. It is always fun to play a game of fetch with your dog, and there are balls and flying discs that are specially made to withstand dog teeth.

COLLAR

Your pup should get used to wearing a collar all the time since you will want to attach his ID tags to it. Plus, you have to attach the lead to something! A lightweight nylon collar is a good choice; make sure that it fits snugly enough so that the pup cannot wriggle out of it, but is loose enough so that it will not be uncomfortably tight around the pup's neck. You should be able to fit a finger between the pup and the collar. It may take some time for your pup to get used to wearing the collar, but soon he will not even notice that it is there. Choke collars should *not* be used on coated or small dogs like the Lhasa.

Most trainers recommend using a lightweight nylon lead for your Lhasa Apso. Pet shops offer dozens of choices for collars and leads, in different styles, colors and lengths.

FINANCIAL RESPONSIBILITY

Grooming tools, collars, leads, a crate, dog beds and, of course, toys will be expenses to you when you first obtain your pup, and the cost will continue throughout your dog's lifetime. If your puppy damages or destroys your possessions (as most puppies surely will!) or something belonging to a neighbor, you can calculate additional expense. There is also flea and pest control, which every dog owner faces more than once. You must be able to handle the financial responsibility of owning a dog.

FOOD AND WATER BOWLS

Your pup will need two bowls, one for food and one for water. You may want two sets of bowls, one for inside and one for outside, depending on where the dog will be spending time. Stainless steel or sturdy plastic bowls are popular choices. Plastic bowls are more chewable. Dogs tend not to chew on the steel variety, which can be sterilized. It is important to buy sturdy bowls since anything is in danger of being chewed by puppy teeth and you do not want your dog to be constantly chewing apart his bowl (for his safety and for your purse!).

CLEANING SUPPLIES

Until a pup is house-trained, you will be doing a lot of cleaning. "Accidents" will occur, which is

The BUCKLE COLLAR is the standard collar used for everyday purposes. Be sure that you adjust the buckle on growing puppies. Check it every day. It can become too tight overnight! These collars can be made of leather or nylon. Attach your dog's identification tags to this collar.

The CHOKE CHAIN is designed for training. It is constructed of highly polished steel so that it slides easily through the stainless steel loop. The idea is that the dog controls the pressure around his neck and he will stop pulling if the collar becomes uncomfortable. *Never* use a choke collar on a Lhasa Apso.

The HALTER is for a trained dog that has to be restrained to prevent running away, chasing a cat and the like. Considered the most humane of all collars, it is frequently used on smaller dogs for which collars are not comfortable.

okay in the beginning because the puppy does not know any better. All you can do is be prepared to clean up any accidents. Paper towels, rags, newspapers and a safe disinfectant are good to have on hand.

BEYOND THE BASICS

The items previously discussed are the bare necessities. You will find out what else you need as you go along—grooming supplies, flea/tick protection, baby gates to partition a room, etc. These things will vary depending on your situation, but it is important that you have everything you need to feed

Tying the Apso's head furnishings back will avoid soiling the hair when he eats or takes a drink.

and make your Lhasa Apso comfortable in his first few days at home.

PUPPY-PROOFING YOUR HOME

Aside from making sure that your Lhasa Apso will be comfortable in your home, you also have to make sure that your home is safe for your Lhasa Apso. This means taking precautions that your pup will not get into anything he should not get into and that there is nothing within his reach that may harm him should he sniff it, chew it, inspect it, etc. This probably seems obvious since, while you are primarily concerned with your pup's safety, at the same time you do not want your belongings to be ruined. Breakables should be placed out of reach if your dog is to have full run of the house. If he is to be limited to certain places within the house, keep any potentially dangerous items in the off-limits areas. An electrical cord can pose a danger should the puppy decide to taste it—and who is going to convince a pup that it would not make a great chew toy? Cords should be fastened tightly against the wall, out of the dog's reach. If your dog is going to spend time in a crate, make sure that there is nothing near his crate that he can reach if he sticks his curious little nose or paws through the openings. Just as you would with a child, keep all household cleaners

Responsible, law-abiding dog owners pick up their dogs' dropping whenever they are in public. Pooper-scooper devices make the job quick and easy.

and chemicals where the pup cannot get to them.

It is also important to make sure that the outside of your home is safe. Of course, your puppy should never be unsupervised, but a pup let loose in the yard will want to run and explore, and he should be granted that freedom. Do not let a fence give you a false sense of security; you would be surprised how crafty (and persistent) a dog can be in figuring out how to dig under and squeeze his way through small holes, or to jump or climb over a fence. The remedy is to make the fence high enough so that it really is impossible for your dog to get over it (about 6 feet should suffice), and well embedded into the ground. Be sure to secure any gaps in the fence. Check the fence periodically to ensure that it is in good shape

Your local pet shop will probably have a wide range of food and water bowls.

Get everything you need before you bring your new puppy home. Your puppy's first night in his new home will be memorable for both you and the puppy.

or maybe you know some other Lhasa Apso owners who can suggest a good vet. Either way, you should have an appointment arranged for your pup before you pick him up and plan on taking him for an examination before or soon after bringing him home.

The pup's first visit will consist of an overall examination to make sure that the pup does not have any problems that are not apparent to you. The veterinarian will also set up a schedule for the pup's vaccinations; the breeder will inform you of which ones the pup has already received and the vet can continue from there.

and make repairs as needed; a very determined pup may return to the same spot to "work on it" until he is able to get through. Some Apsos are skilled climbers and will surprise their owners by getting over fencing of more-than-ample height.

FIRST TRIP TO THE VET

You have picked out your puppy, and your home and family are ready. Now all you have to do is collect your Lhasa Apso from the breeder and the fun begins, right? Well…not so fast. Something else you need to prepare is your pup's first trip to the veterinarian. Perhaps the breeder can recommend someone in the area who specializes in Lhasa Apsos,

CHEMICAL TOXINS

Thoroughly puppy-proof your house before bringing your puppy home. Never use cockroach or rodent poisons or plant fertilizers in any area accessible to the puppy. Avoid the use of toilet cleaners. Most dogs are born with "toilet-bowl sonar" and will take a drink if the lid is left open. Also keep the trash secured and out of reach.

Scour your garage for potential puppy dangers. Remove weed killers, pesticides and antifreeze materials. Antifreeze is highly toxic and just a few drops can kill a puppy or an adult dog. The sweet taste attracts the animal, who will quickly consume it from the floor or pavement.

The yard should be secure so the Apso can go out to relieve himself and enjoy supervised free play without the danger of his getting loose.

INTRODUCTION TO THE FAMILY

Everyone in the house will be excited about the puppy's coming home and will want to pet him and play with him, but it is best to make the introduction low-key so as not to overwhelm the puppy. He is apprehensive already. It is the first time he has been separated from his mother and the breeder, and the ride to your home is likely the first time he has been in a car. The last thing you want to do is smother him, as this will only frighten him further. This is not to say that human contact is not extremely necessary at this stage, because this is the time when a connection between the pup and his human family is formed. Gentle petting and soothing words should help console him, as well as just putting him down and letting him explore on his own (under your watchful eye, of course).

NATURAL TOXINS

Examine your lawn and home landscaping before bringing your puppy home. Many varieties of plants have leaves, stems or flowers that are toxic if ingested, and you can depend on a curious puppy to investigate them. Ask your vet for information on poisonous plants or research them at your library.

The pup may approach the family members or may busy himself with exploring for a while. Gradually, each person should spend some time with the pup, one at a time, crouching down to get as close to the pup's level as possible and letting him sniff their hands and petting him gently. Do not rush the Apso pup, as the breed can be a little aloof. Just remember that the pup is experiencing a lot of things for the first time, at the same time. There are new people, new noises, new smells and new things to investigate, so be gentle, be affectionate and be as comforting as you can be.

THE RIDE HOME

Taking your dog from the breeder to your home in a car can be a very uncomfortable experience for both of you. The puppy will have been taken from his warm, friendly, safe environment and brought into a strange new environment—an environment that moves! Be prepared for loose bowels, urination, crying, whining and even fear biting. With proper love and encouragement when you arrive home, the stress of the trip should quickly disappear.

YOUR PUP'S FIRST NIGHT HOME

You have traveled home with your new charge safely in his crate or on a family member's lap. He's been to the vet for a thorough check-up; he's been weighed, his papers examined; perhaps he's even been vaccinated and wormed as well. He's explored his area, his new crate, the yard and anywhere else he's been permitted. He's eaten his first meal at home and relieved himself in the proper place. He's heard lots of new sounds, smelled new friends and seen more of the outside world than ever before.

That was just the first day! He's worn out and is ready for bed...or so you think!

It's puppy's first night and you are ready to say "Good night"— keep in mind that this is puppy's first night ever to be sleeping alone. His dam and littermates are no longer at paw's length and he's a bit scared, cold and lonely. Be reassuring to your new family member, but this is not the time to spoil him and give in to his inevitable whining.

Puppies whine. They whine to let others know where they are and hopefully to get company out of it. Place your pup in his new bed or crate in his room and close the crate door. Mercifully, he may fall asleep without a peep. When the inevitable occurs, ignore the whining: he is fine. Be strong and keep his interest in mind. Do not allow your heart to become guilty and visit the pup. He will fall asleep.

Many breeders recommend placing a piece of bedding from the pup's former home in his new bed so that he recognizes the scent of his littermates. Others still advise placing a hot water bottle in his bed for warmth. This latter may be a good idea provided the pup doesn't attempt to suckle—he'll get good and wet and may not fall asleep so fast.

Puppy's first night can be somewhat stressful for the pup and his new family. Remember that you are setting the tone of nighttime at your house. Unless you want to play with your pup every night at 10 p.m., midnight and 2 a.m., don't initiate the habit. Your family will thank you, and eventually so will your pup!

PREVENTING PUPPY PROBLEMS

SOCIALIZATION
Now that you have done all of the preparatory work and have helped your pup get accustomed to his new home and family, it is about time for you to have some fun! Socializing your Lhasa Apso pup gives you the opportunity to show off your new friend, and your pup gets to reap the benefits of being an adorable furry creature that people will want to pet and, in

general, think is absolutely precious!

Besides getting to know his new family, your puppy should be exposed to other people, animals and situations, but of course he must not come into close contact with dogs you don't know well until his course of injections is fully completed. Socialization will help the pup

A basket with nice pillow is an excellent choice for the new puppy. Offer the puppy a safe chew toy to take to his new bed.

TRAINING TIP

Training your puppy takes much patience and can be frustrating at times, but you should see results from your efforts. If you have a puppy that seems untrainable, take him to a trainer or behaviorist. The dog may have a personality problem that requires the help of a professional, or perhaps you need help in learning how to train your dog.

An Apso with his Miniature Schnauzer friend. Early socialization produces dogs that get along well with other dogs and animals.

An Apso with his Miniature Schnauzer friend. Early socialization produces dogs that get along well with other dogs and animals.

become well adjusted as he grows up and less prone to being timid or fearful of the new things he will encounter. Your pup's socialization began at the breeder's, but now it is your responsibility to continue it. The socialization he receives after going to his new home is the most critical, as this is the time when he forms his impressions of the outside world. Be especially careful during the first couple of weeks at home. The interaction he receives during this time should be gentle and reassuring. Lack of socialization can manifest itself in fear and aggression

as the dog grows up. He needs lots of human contact, affection, handling and exposure to other animals.

Once your pup has received his necessary vaccinations, feel free to take him out and about (on

IN DUE TIME

It will take at least two weeks for your puppy to become accustomed to his new surroundings. Give him lots of love, attention, handling, frequent opportunities to relieve himself, a diet he likes to eat and a place he can call his own.

his lead, of course). Walk him around the neighborhood, take him on your daily errands, let people pet him, let him meet other dogs and pets, etc. Puppies do not have to try to make friends; there will be no shortage of people who will want to introduce themselves. Just make sure that you carefully supervise each meeting. If the neighborhood children want to say hello, for example, that is fine, but be cautious. Sometimes an excited child can unintentionally handle a pup too roughly, or an overzealous pup can playfully nip a little too hard. You want to make socialization experiences positive ones. What a pup learns during this very formative stage will impact his attitude toward future encounters. You want your dog to be comfortable around everyone. A pup that has a bad experience with a child may grow up to be a dog that is shy around or aggressive toward children.

DOG MEETS WORLD

Thorough socialization includes not only meeting new people and other pets but also being introduced to new experiences such as riding in the car, having his coat brushed, hearing the television, walking in a crowd—the list is endless. The more your Apso experiences, and the more positive the experiences are, the less of a shock and the less frightening it will be for your dog to encounter new things.

Lhasa Apsos, when properly fed and cared for, stay in remarkable condition throughout their lives. This youthful-looking Apso is 12 years old and looking like a pup!

CONSISTENCY IN TRAINING

Dogs, being pack animals, naturally need a leader, or else they try to establish dominance in their packs. When you bring a dog into your family, the choice of who becomes the leader and who becomes the "pack" is entirely up to you! Your pup's intuitive quest for dominance, coupled with the fact that it is nearly impossible to resist an adorable Lhasa Apso pup, give the pup almost an unfair advantage in getting the upper hand! A pup will definitely test the waters to see what he can and cannot do. Do not give in to those pleading eyes—stand your ground when it comes to disciplining the pup and make sure that all family members do the same. It will only confuse the pup when Mother tells him to get off the couch when he is used to sitting up there with Father to watch the nightly news. Avoid discrepancies by having all members of the household decide on the rules before the pup even comes home...and be consistent in

MENTAL AND DENTAL

Toys not only help your puppy get the physical and mental stimulation he needs but also provide a great way to keep his teeth clean. Hard rubber or nylon toys, especially those constructed with grooves, are designed to scrape away plaque, preventing bad breath and gum infection.

enforcing them! Early training shapes the dog's personality, so you cannot be unclear in what you expect.

COMMON PUPPY PROBLEMS

The best way to prevent puppy problems is to be proactive in stopping an undesirable behavior as soon as it starts. The old saying "You can't teach an old dog new tricks" does not necessarily hold true, but it *is* true that it is much easier to discourage bad behavior in a young developing pup than to wait until the pup's bad behavior becomes the adult dog's bad habit. There are some problems that are especially prevalent in puppies as they develop.

NIPPING

As puppies start to teethe, they feel the need to sink their teeth into anything available…unfortunately, that includes your fingers, arms, hair and toes. You may find this behavior cute for the first five seconds…until you feel just how sharp those puppy teeth are. This is something you want to discourage immediately and consistently with a firm "No!" (or whatever number of firm "Nos" it takes for him to understand that you mean business). Then replace your finger with an appropriate chew toy. While this behavior is merely annoying when the dog is young, it can become dangerous as your Lhasa Apso's adult teeth grow in and his jaws develop, and he continues to think it is okay to gnaw on human appendages.

CRYING/WHINING

Your pup will often cry, whine, whimper, howl or make some type

---

CHEWING TIPS

Chewing goes hand in hand with nipping in the sense that a teething puppy is always looking for a way to soothe his aching gums. In this case, instead of chewing on you, he may have taken a liking to your favorite shoe or something else that he should not be chewing. Again, realize that this is a normal canine behavior that does not need to be discouraged, only redirected. Your pup just needs to be taught what is acceptable to chew on and what is off-limits. Consistently tell him "No!" when you catch him chewing on something forbidden and give him a chew toy.

Conversely, praise him when you catch him chewing on something appropriate. In this way, you are discouraging the inappropriate behavior and reinforcing the desired behavior. The puppy's chewing should stop after his adult teeth have come in, but an adult dog continues to chew for various reasons—perhaps because he is bored, needs to relieve tension or just likes to chew. That is why it is important to redirect his chewing when he is still young.

Cold weather need not deter your housebreaking routine, though a warm sweater may be welcomed by some Apsos.

Cold weather need not deter your housebreaking routine, though a warm sweater may be welcomed by some Apsos.

Opposite page: Litters are usually raised in wire pens or similar areas; as they grow, they need to be taught to leave their area for toileting purposes.

of commotion when he is left alone. This is basically his way of calling out for attention to make sure that you know he is there and that you have not forgotten about him. He feels insecure when he is left alone, when you are out of the house and he is in his crate or when you are in another part of the house and he cannot see you.

PUPPY PROBLEMS

The majority of problems that are commonly seen in young pups will disappear as your dog gets older. However, how you deal with problems when he is young will determine how he reacts to discipline as an adult dog. It is important to establish who is boss (hopefully it will be you!) right away when you are first bonding with your dog. This bond will set the tone for the rest of your life together.

The noise he is making is an expression of the anxiety he feels at being alone, so he needs to be taught that being alone is okay. You are not actually training the dog to stop making noise, you are training him to feel comfortable when he is alone and thus removing the need for him to make the noise. This is where the crate filled with cozy bedding and a favorite toy comes in handy. You want to know that he is safe when you are not there to supervise, and you know that he will be safe in his crate rather than roaming freely about the house. In order for the pup to stay in his crate without making a fuss, he needs to be comfortable in his crate. On that note, it is extremely important that the crate is never used as a form of punishment, or the pup will have a negative association with the crate.

Accustom the pup to the crate in short, gradually increasing time intervals in which you put him in the crate, maybe with a treat, and stay in the room with him. If he cries or makes a fuss, do not go to him, but stay in his sight. Gradually he will realize that staying in his crate is okay without your help, and it will not be so traumatic for him when you are not around. You may want to leave the radio on softly when you leave the house; the sound of human voices may be comforting to him.

LHASA APSO

DIETARY AND FEEDING CONSIDERATIONS

Today the choices of food for your Lhasa Apso are many and varied. There are simply dozens of brands of food in all sorts of flavors, ranging from puppy diets to those for seniors. There are even hypoallergenic and low-calorie diets available. Because your Lhasa Apso's food has a bearing on his coat, health and temperament, it is essential that the most suitable diet is selected for a Lhasa Apso of his age. It is fair to say, however, that even dedicated owners can be somewhat perplexed by the enormous range of foods available. Only understanding what is best for your dog will help you reach a valued decision.

Dog foods are produced in three basic types: dry, semi-moist and canned. Dry foods are useful for the cost-conscious for overall they tend to be less expensive than semi-moist or canned. These contain the least fat and the most preservatives. In general, canned foods are made up of 60–70% water, while semi-moist ones often contain so much sugar that they are perhaps the least

FOOD PREFERENCE

Selecting the best dry dog food is difficult. There is no majority consensus among veterinary scientists as to the value of nutrient analyses (protein, fat, fiber, moisture, ash, cholesterol, minerals, etc.). All agree that feeding trials are what matter most, but you also have to consider the individual dog. The dog's weight, age and activity level, and what pleases his taste, all must be considered. It is probably best to take the advice of your veterinarian. Every dog's dietary requirements vary, even during the lifetime of a particular dog.

If your dog is fed a good dry food, it does not require supplements of meat or vegetables. Dogs do appreciate a little variety in their diets, so you may choose to stay with the same brand but vary the flavor. Alternatively, you may wish to add a little flavored stock to give a difference to the taste.

Lhasa Apso puppies enjoy a milk feed as part of their weaning process.

preferred by owners, even though their dogs seem to like them.

When selecting your dog's diet, three stages of development must be considered: the puppy stage, the adult stage and the senior stage.

PUPPY STAGE

Puppies instinctively want to suck milk from their mother's teats, and a normal puppy will exhibit this behavior from just a few moments following birth. If puppies do not attempt to suckle within the first half-hour or so, the breeder should encourage them to do so by placing them on the nipples, having selected ones with plenty of milk. This early milk supply is important in providing colostrum to protect the puppies during the first eight to ten weeks of their lives. Although a mother's milk is much better than any milk formula, despite there being some excellent ones available, if the puppies do not feed, the breeder will have to feed them himself. For those with less experience, advice from a veterinarian is important so that not only the right quantity of milk is fed but also that of correct quality, fed at suitably frequent intervals, usually every two hours during the first few days of life.

Puppies should be allowed to nurse from their mothers for about the first six weeks, although from the third or fourth week the

Feeding the Lhasa Apso is more complicated than placing a bowl of food on the floor at suppertime. You must find out which food is best for your dog, based on his breeding, activity level, environment and other factors.

breeder will begin to introduce small portions of suitable solid food. Most breeders like to introduce alternate milk and meat meals initially, building up to weaning time.

TEST FOR PROPER DIET

A good test for proper diet is the color, odor and firmness of your dog's stool. A healthy dog usually produces three semi-hard stools per day. The stools should have no unpleasant odor. They should be the same color from excretion to excretion.

By the time the puppies are seven or a maximum of eight weeks old, they should be fully weaned and fed solely on a proprietary puppy food. Selection of the most suitable, good-quality diet at this time is essential, for a puppy's fastest growth rate is during the first year of life. Veterinarians are usually able to offer advice in this regard and, although the frequency of meals will be reduced over time, only when a young dog has reached the age of about 18 months should an adult diet be fed.

Puppy and junior diets should be well balanced for the needs of your dog, so that except in certain circumstances additional vitamins, minerals and proteins will not be required.

GRAIN-BASED DIETS

Some less expensive dog foods are based on grains and other plant proteins. While these products may appear to be attractively priced, many breeders prefer a diet based on animal proteins and believe that they are more conducive to your dog's health. Many grain-based diets rely on soy protein, which may cause flatulence (passing gas).

There are many cases, however, when your dog might require a special diet. These special requirements should only be recommended by your veterinarian.

ADULT DIETS

A dog is considered an adult when it has stopped growing, so in general the diet of a Lhasa Apso can be changed to an adult one at about 18 months of age. Again you should rely upon your veterinarian or breeder to recommend an acceptable maintenance diet. Major dog-food manufacturers specialize in this type of food, and it is just necessary for you to select the one best suited to your dog's needs. Active dogs may have different requirements than sedate dogs.

SENIOR DIETS

As dogs get older, their metabolism changes. The older dog usually exercises less, moves more slowly and sleeps more. This change in lifestyle and physiological performance requires a change in diet. Since these changes take place slowly, they might not be recognizable. What is easily recognizable is weight gain. By continuing to feed your dog an adult-maintenance diet when he is slowing down metabolically, your dog will gain weight. Obesity in an older dog compounds the health problems that already accompany old age.

As your dog gets older, few of his organs function up to par. The kidneys slow down and the intestines become less efficient. These age-related factors are best handled with a change in diet and

A Worthy Investment

Veterinary studies have proven that a balanced
high-quality diet pays off in your dog's coat quality,
behavior and activity level. Invest in premium
brands for the maximum payoff with your dog.

Your local pet shop will probably have a wide assortment of grooming tools to enable you to keep your Apso in magnificent coat.

a change in feeding schedule to give smaller portions that are more easily digested.

There is no single best diet for every older dog. While many dogs do well on light or senior diets, other dogs do better on puppy diets or other special premium diets such as lamb and rice. Be sensitive to your senior Lhasa Apso's diet and this will help control other problems that may arise with your old friend.

WATER

Just as your dog needs proper nutrition from his food, water is an essential "nutrient" as well. Water keeps the dog's body properly hydrated and promotes normal function of the body's systems. During housebreaking, it is necessary to keep an eye on how much water your Lhasa Apso is drinking, but once he is reliably trained he should have access to clean, fresh water at all times. Make sure that the dog's water bowl is clean, and change the water often, making sure that water is always available for your dog, especially if you feed dry food.

EXERCISE

Although a Lhasa Apso is small, all dogs require some form of exercise, regardless of breed. A sedentary lifestyle is as harmful to a dog as it is to a person. The Lhasa Apso enjoys exercise, but

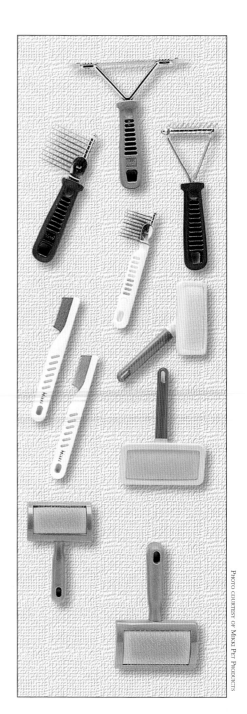

you don't have to be an Olympic athlete to give him the activity he needs. Regular walks, play sessions in the yard or letting the dog run free in the yard under your supervision are sufficient forms of exercise for the Lhasa Apso. For those who are more ambitious, you will find that your Lhasa Apso can keep up with you on long walks or an occasional hike! Bear in mind that an over-weight dog should never be suddenly over-exercised; instead, he should be allowed to increase exercise slowly. Not only is exer-cise essential to keep the dog's body fit, it is essential to his mental well-being. A bored dog will find something to do, which often manifests itself in some type of destructive behavior. In this sense, it is essential for the owner's mental well-being as well!

GROOMING

Your Lhasa Apso will need to be groomed regularly, so it is essen-tial that short grooming sessions are introduced from a very early age. From the beginning, a few minutes each day should be set aside. The duration should build up slowly as the puppy matures and the coat grows in length. Your puppy should be taught to stand on a solid surface for grooming—a suitable table on which the dog will not slip. Under no circumstances leave

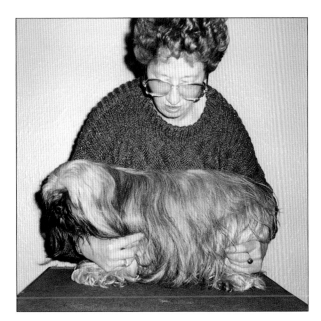

your Apso alone on a table for he may all too easily jump off and injure himself. A commercially made grooming table, equipped with rubber matting, a noose and a grooming arm, makes an excel-lent investment for the Lhasa owner.

When the puppy is used to standing on the table, you will need to teach him to be rolled over onto his side. This you will do by grasping his front and back legs on the opposite side of your own body, then gently placing him down by leaning over him for reassurance. To begin, just stroke his tummy so that he looks upon this new routine as something highly pleasurable. Then, when you know he is comfortable with this, introduce a few gentle brush

The process of putting an Apso over on his side to be groomed begins with grasping the dog's legs and gently rolling him onto his side on the grooming table.

strokes. Be sure you don't tug at any knots at this stage, for this would cause him to associate the grooming routine with pain. This may take a little getting used to both for you and your puppy, but only if your Apso learns to lie down on his side will you easily be able to groom in all the awkward places. You will both be glad you had a little patience to learn this trick from the very start!

You will notice that your Lhasa Apso's coat grows longer with age. Usually between 10 and 12 months, the coat changes from a puppy coat to an adult one. This will be a difficult time when knots will form very easily, and you will realize how comparatively easy it was to groom the puppy coat!

You will certainly need to groom the coat between bath times, but never groom the coat when completely dry. To avoid breaking the ends, use a light conditioning spray; even water dispensed from a fine-spray bottle is better than no moisture at all.

ROUTINE GROOMING

With your Lhasa Apso lying on his side, the coat should be parted, layered and brushed section by section, always in the direction of the coat growth. It is imperative to groom right down to the skin so that the undercoat does not become matted. After using a good-quality bristle brush, a wide-toothed comb can be used to finish each section.

If you do find mats in your Apso's coat, spray the mat with a generous amount of conditioning or anti-tangle spray. Leave this to soak in for a few moments, then gently tease out the mat with your fingers. Always work from the inside out, or the knot will just get tighter! Tight knots will probably need to be teased out using a wide-toothed comb, but don't tug at the knot for this will be painful and will also take out too much coat.

GROOMING EQUIPMENT

How much grooming equipment you purchase will depend on how much grooming you are going to do yourself. Here are some basics:

- Grooming table
- Natural bristle brush
- Metal comb
- Scissors
- Conditioning spray
- Dental elastics
- Spray hose attachment
- Blow dryer
- Rubber mat
- Dog shampoo
- Conditioner
- Towels
- Ear cleaner
- Cotton balls
- Ear tweezers
- Nail clippers

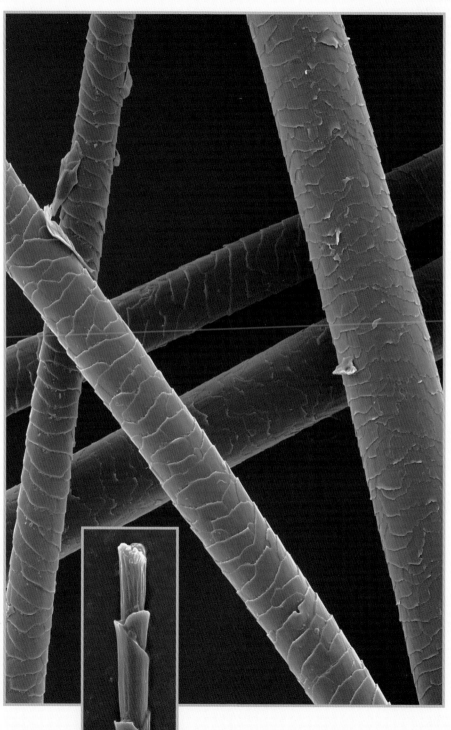

Healthy dog hairs enlarged about 200 times their natural size. The inset shows the tip of a growing hair.

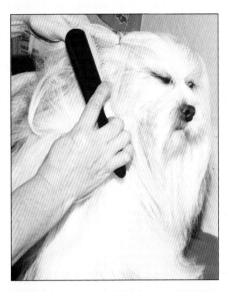

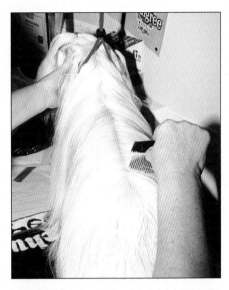

Brushing the coat thoroughly removes any mats and tangles. Brushing is necessary both before bathing and after the coat is completely dry.

A straight part is made, starting at the dog's head and running the entire length of the back.

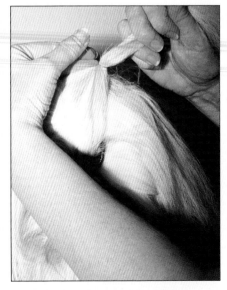

Combing follows brushing, using a fine-toothed metal comb.

The hair is tied back on each side with a light elastic band, taking care not to pull the hair too tightly.

The hair is trimmed uniformly at ground level, using the grooming table as a guide.

Take care grooming the tummy and under the "armpits," for these areas are especially sensitive. There is really no harm in cutting away small tight knots from under the armpits, as these will not show and the dog will feel more comfortable.

Because a Lhasa Apso's coat just seems to keep on growing, it is usually necessary to trim the coat at ground level. To do this neatly, stand your dog on the edge of a table and, using hair-dressing scissors, carefully cut off the hair that hangs below the edge of the table. This will leave a nice straight line around the bottom of the coat. Trimming below the pads of the feet

All of the grooming effort pays off when you see the results: a Lhasa Apso with a beautiful coat.

The hair should be removed from in between the foot pads to prevent uncomfortable hairballs from forming.

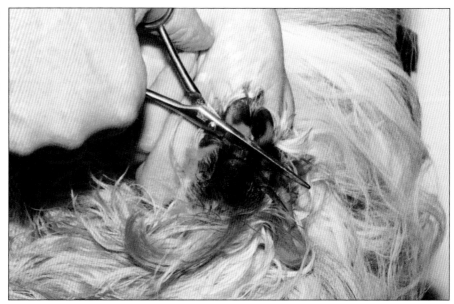

prevents uncomfortable hairballs from forming between the pads. On males, most owners also trim off a little hair from the end of the penis, but a good half-inch or so must be left so that tiny hairs do not aggravate the penis and cause infection. Whatever you do, take care not to cut through a nipple, and remember that males have little nipples too!

The legs and "pants" of a Lhasa Apso are very heavily coated and will also need regular grooming. To prevent knots and tangles, be sure to immediately remove any debris that may have accumulated following a visit outdoors. Also always check your dog's back end to see that nothing remains attached to the coat from his bowel movement. Between baths, you

may like to use a damp sponge, but always be sure to dry the coat thoroughly. Drying will keep your Apso comfortable and will prevent the coat from curling too much.

Some Lhasa Apsos don't seem to mind having their feet groomed, while others hate it. Nonetheless, you will have to check the feet thoroughly on a regular basis. Be sure you don't allow knots to build up between the toes, and always keep an eye on the length of the toenails.

THE HEAD AND THE FINISHING TOUCHES

It is essential to keep the whiskers, beard and eyes of a Lhasa Apso clean, so these must be checked every day. Eyes can be cleaned with a liquid eye cleaner made for dogs. The beard and whiskers can be washed and combed through, and some owners find it useful to attach small elastic bands on each side of the beard to prevent soiling, especially when the dog is eating.

When grooming, pay special attention to the hair behind the ears—this is often of a finer texture and knots easily. When not in the show ring, owners often like to tie the head hair with tiny elastic bands on each side of the head. Most owners use dental elastics, but take care not to pull up the hair too tightly so that it pulls on the eyes. Elastics will generally need to be changed at least once a day. Never pull them out; always cut them carefully with scissors so as not to damage any hair. Under no circumstances should the head hair be trimmed for the show ring, although, if a Lhasa Apso is maintained in pet trim, the head hair can be cut short to match the rest of the coat. Some pet owners, though, like to keep long fringing on the ears. When grooming is complete, take a wide-toothed comb to create a straight parting down the length of the back so that the coat falls evenly on either side.

BATHING AND DRYING

How frequently you decide to bathe your Lhasa Apso will depend very much on whether

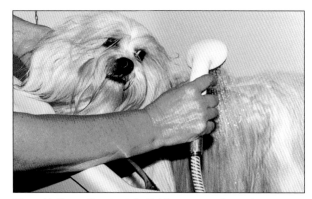

The coat is thoroughly saturated with lukewarm water from a shower attachment.

Dog shampoo is applied to the dog's coat, keeping it away from the Lhasa's eyes. Apply the shampoo by stroking, as rubbing creates knots.

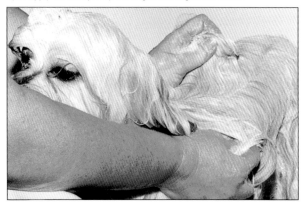

Shampoo is gently worked into a lather and the suds massaged all the way to the skin.

All of the hard-to-reach places should be thoroughly cleaned.

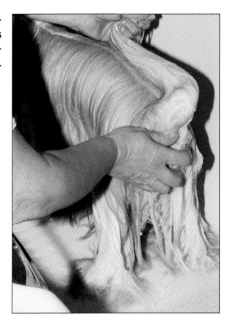

After the dog is rinsed, he is wrapped in a soft towel and lifted from the tub.

your dog is a show dog or a pet. Show dogs are usually bathed before every show, which may be as frequent as once a week. Pet dogs are usually bathed less frequently, especially if they are kept in puppy trim because the coat does not drag on the ground to pick up dirt and debris.

Every owner has his own preference as to how best to bathe, but ideally the coat should be groomed through before bathing. I like to stand my own dogs on a non-slip mat in the bathtub or sink, then wet the coat thoroughly using a shower attachment. It is imperative that the water temperature is first tested on your own hand. Use a good-quality shampoo designed especially for dogs, always stroking it into the coat rather than rubbing, so as not to create knots. When this has been thoroughly rinsed out, apply a canine conditioner in the same manner, then rinse again until the water runs clear. Many people like to use a baby shampoo on the head to avoid irritation to the eyes, and some like to plug the ears with cotton balls to avoid water getting inside. Personally, I use neither of these; instead I just take special care in those areas, and I have never encountered problems.

Before taking your dog out of the bath, it is a good idea to use a highly absorbent hand towel to soak up excess moisture. Remove

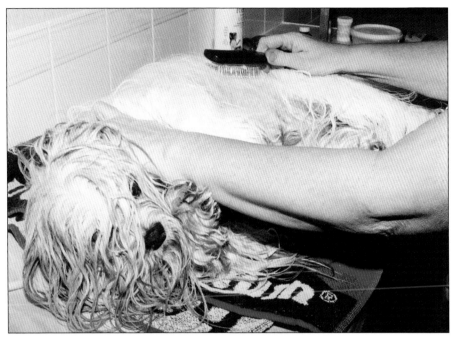

Post-bath brushing on the grooming table is done while using a hair dryer on a low heat setting to keep the coat free of tangles while drying.

your Apso from the bath by wrapping him in a clean towel and lifting him out. Undoubtedly your dog will want to shake—so be prepared!

Drying can be done on the same table that you use for the grooming process. Work systematically, all the while brushing as well as applying warm (not hot) air from the hair dryer.

Never just blow-dry the dog with the intention of grooming later, or your Lhasa Apso's coat will not end up looking in good condition. Certainly never allow an Apso to dry naturally.

Put the finishing touches to your dog's coat, just as you would have done if grooming without a

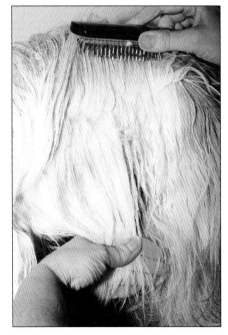

Brush the hair in the direction in which it lays.

Cleaning an Apso's ears on a regular basis is very important. Use an ear cleansing solution (available from your vet or pet shop) with a cotton ball. Clean gently, *never* probing into the ear canal.

The long hairs growing in the Apso's ears should be removed by pulling only a few hairs at a time. This is painless if it is done properly.

bath. Bathing and grooming a long-coated breed is always a lengthy task but, I assure you, the end result will make it all worthwhile.

EAR CLEANING

Because the Lhasa Apso has such a long coat, long hair will also grow inside the ears. This should carefully be plucked out either with special blunt-ended tweezers or, if you prefer, with your fingertips. By always removing only a few hairs at a time, the procedure should be entirely painless.

Ears should be kept clean. This can be done with a cotton ball and special cleaner or ear powder made especially for dogs. Be on the lookout for any signs of infection or ear-mite infestation. If your Lhasa Apso has been shaking his head or scratching at his ears frequently, this usually indicates a problem. If his ears have an unusual odor, this is a sure sign of mite infestation or infection, and a signal to have his ears checked by the veterinarian.

NAIL CLIPPING

Your Lhasa Apso should be accustomed to having his nails trimmed at an early age, since it will be part of your maintenance routine throughout his life. Long nails can all too easily get caught in the Lhasa Apso's long coat, and can scratch someone unintentionally.

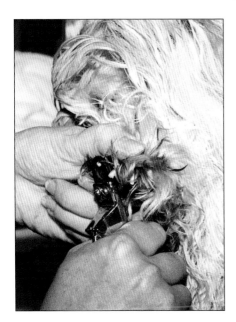

Canine Pedicure

Nail Casing

Quick

Cut Line

Dark-colored nail

With black or dark nails, it's best to clip only the tip of the nail or to use a file.

Light-colored nail

In light-colored nails, clipping is much simpler because you can see the vein (or quick) that grows inside the casing.

Your Apso's nails should be trimmed regularly. When you can hear the nails clicking as the dog walks on a hard surface, the nails are too long. Pet shops sell special clippers for dog's nails.

Also, a long nail has a better chance of ripping and bleeding, or causing the feet to spread. A good rule of thumb is that if you can hear your dog's nails' clicking on the floor when he walks, his nails are too long.

Before you start cutting, make sure you can identify the "quick" in each nail. The quick is a blood vessel that runs through the center of each nail and grows rather close to the end. It will bleed if accidentally cut, which will be quite painful for the dog as it contains nerve endings. Keep some type of clotting agent on hand, such as a styptic pencil or styptic powder (the type used for shaving). This will stop the bleeding quickly when applied to the end of the cut nail. Do not panic if this happens,

Carefully clean around the Apso's eyes to remove tear stains.

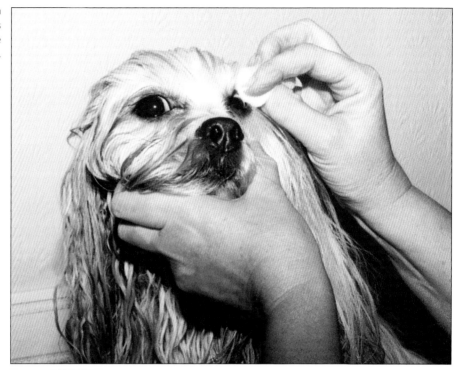

just stop the bleeding and talk soothingly to your dog. Once he has calmed down, move on to the next nail. It is better to clip a little at a time, particularly with black-nailed dogs.

Brush your Apso's teeth regularly; usually a weekly cleaning will suffice.

Hold your pup steady as you begin trimming his nails; you do not want him to make any sudden movements or run away. Talk to him soothingly and stroke him as you clip. Holding his foot in your hand, simply take off the end of each nail with one quick clip. You can purchase nail clippers that are specially made for dogs; you can probably find them wherever you buy pet or grooming supplies.

TRAVELING WITH YOUR DOG

CAR TRAVEL
You should accustom your Lhasa Apso to riding in a car at an early age. You may or may not take him

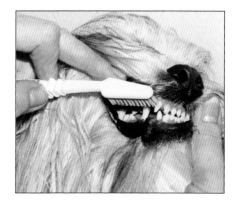

in the car often, but at the very least he will need to go to the vet and you do not want these trips to be traumatic for the dog or a big hassle for you. The safest way for a dog to ride in the car is in his crate. If he uses a crate in the house, you can use the same crate for travel.

Put the pup in the crate and see how he reacts. If he seems uneasy, you can have a passenger hold him on his lap while you drive. Another option is a specially made safety harness for dogs, which straps the dog in much like a seat belt. Do not let the dog roam loose in the vehicle—this is very dangerous! If you should stop short, your dog can be thrown and injured. If the dog starts climbing on you and pestering you while you are driving, you will not be able to concentrate on the road. It is an unsafe situation for everyone—human and canine.

For long trips, be prepared to stop to let the dog relieve himself. Bring along whatever you need to

clean up after him. You should take along some old rags or paper towels for use should he have a potty accident in the car or suffer from motion sickness.

LHASAS IN THE FRIENDLY SKIES
Contact your chosen airline before proceeding with travel plans that include your Lhasa Apso. The dog will be required to travel in a fiberglass crate and you should always check in advance with the airline regarding specific requirements for the crate's size, type and labeling. To help put the dog at ease, give him one of his favorite toys in the crate. Do not feed the dog for several hours prior to checking in so that you minimize his need to relieve himself. Some airlines require you to provide documentation as to when the dog has last been fed. In any case, a light meal is the best option.

Make sure that your dog is properly identified and that your

The most acceptable, safest way of traveling with your Lhasa Apso in a car is with the dog in his crate. It is dangerous for the dog to roam free in the vehicle while it is moving.

TRAVEL TIP

Never leave your dog alone in the car. In hot weather, your dog can die from the high temperature inside a closed vehicle; even a car parked in the shade can heat up very quickly. Leaving the window open is dangerous as well since the dog can hurt himself trying to get out.

An elderly Lhasa Apso enjoys a nap on her master's favorite chair. Are you prepared to care for your dog through all stages of life?

GOING ABROAD

For international travel, you will have to make arrangements well in advance (perhaps months), as countries' regulations pertaining to bringing in animals differ. There may be special health certificates and/or vaccinations that your dog will need before taking the trip; sometimes this has to be done within a certain time frame. When traveling to rabies-free countries, you will need to bring proof of the dog's rabies vaccination and there will likely be a quarantine period upon arrival.

contact information appears on his ID tags and on his crate. Although most dogs travel in a different area of the plane than the human passengers, the Lhasa Apso maybe fortunate enough to travel in "coach" (or "first-class") along with his owners! Most airlines provide for small dogs to travel with their owners, and Lhasa Apso owners should always see if their dogs qualify for in-cabin travel.

BOARDING AND VACATIONS
So you want to take a family vacation—and you want to include *all* members of the family. You would probably make arrangements for accommodations ahead of time anyway, but this is especially important when travel-

Should you find it necessary to board your Lhasa Apso while you are on vacation, locate a facility with clean accommodations and a friendly, knowledgeable staff.

ing with a dog. You do not want to make an overnight stop at the only place around for miles and find out that they do not allow dogs. Also, you do not want to reserve a place for your family without confirming that you are traveling with a dog because, if it is against their policy, you may not have a place to stay.

Alternatively, if you are traveling and choose not to bring your Lhasa Apso, you will have to make arrangements for him while you are away. Some options are to take him to a friend's house to stay while you are gone, to have a trusted neighbor stay at your house or to bring your dog to a reputable boarding kennel. If you choose to board him at a kennel, you should visit in advance to see

COLLAR REQUIRED

If your dog gets lost, he is not able to ask for directions home. Identification tags fastened to the collar give important information—the dog's name, the owner's name, the owner's address and a telephone number where the owner can be reached. This makes it easy for whoever finds the dog to contact the owner and arrange to have the dog returned. An added advantage is that a person will be more likely to approach a lost dog who has ID tags on his collar; it tells the person that this is somebody's pet rather than a stray. This is the easiest and fastest method of identification, provided that the tags stay on the collar and the collar stays on the dog.

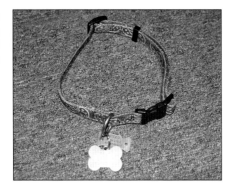

Your Lhasa Apso's ID tags should be securely attached to his collar.

the facility, how clean they are and where the dogs are kept. Talk to some of the employees and see how they treat the dogs—have they experience in grooming long-coated dogs, do they spend time with the dogs, play with them, exercise them, etc.? Also find out the kennel's policy on vaccinations and what they require. This is for all of the dogs' safety, since when dogs are kept together, there is a greater risk of diseases being passed from dog to dog.

IDENTIFICATION

Your Lhasa Apso is your valued companion and friend. That is why you always keep a close eye on him and you have made sure that he cannot escape from the garden or wriggle out of his collar and run away from you. However, accidents can happen and there may come a time when your dog unexpectedly gets separated from you. If this unfortunate event should occur, the first thing on your mind will be finding him. Proper identification, including an ID tag, and possibly a tattoo and/or microchip, will increase the chances of his being returned to you safely and quickly.

IDENTIFICATION OPTIONS

As puppies become more and more expensive, especially those puppies of high quality for showing and/or breeding, they have a greater chance of being stolen. The usual collar dog tag is, of course, easily removed. But there are two more permanent techniques that have become widely used for identification.

The puppy microchip implantation involves the injection of a small microchip, about the size of a corn kernel, under the skin of the dog. If your dog shows up at a clinic or shelter, or is offered for resale under less-than-savory circumstances, it can be positively identified by the microchip. The microchip is scanned, and a registry quickly identifies you as the owner.

Tattooing is done on various parts of the dog, from his belly to his cheeks. The number tattooed can be your telephone number or any other number that you can easily memorize. When professional dog thieves see a tattooed dog, they usually lose interest. For the safety of our dogs, no laboratory facility or dog broker will accept a tattooed dog as stock. Both microchipping and tattooing can be done at your local veterinary clinic.

A dog in pet trim can wear his collar all the time; some owners prefer to remove the collars from dogs in full coat when the dogs are indoors.

Living with an untrained dog is a lot like owning a piano that you do not know how to play—it is a nice object to look at, but it does not do much more than that to bring you pleasure. Now try taking piano lessons, and suddenly the piano comes alive and brings forth magical sounds and rhythms that set your heart singing and your body swaying.

The same is true with your Lhasa Apso. Any dog is a big responsibility and, if not trained sensibly, may develop unacceptable behavior that annoys you or even causes family friction.

To train your Lhasa Apso, you may like to enroll in an obedience class. Teach him good manners as you learn how and why he behaves the way he does. Find out how to communicate with your dog and how to recognize and understand his communications with you. Suddenly the dog takes on a new role in your life—he is smart, interesting, well behaved and fun to be with. He demonstrates his bond of devotion to you daily. In other words, your Lhasa Apso does wonders for your ego because he constantly reminds you that you are not only his leader, you are his hero!

Those involved with teaching dog obedience and counseling owners about their dogs' behavior have discovered some interesting facts about dog ownership. For example, training dogs when they are puppies results in the highest rate of success in developing well-mannered and well-adjusted adult dogs. Training an older dog, from six months to six years of age, can produce almost equal results, providing that the owner accepts the dog's slower rate of learning capability and is willing to work patiently to help the dog succeed at developing to his fullest potential. Unfortunately, many owners of untrained adult dogs lack the patience factor, so they do not persist until their dogs are successful at learning particular behaviors.

REAP THE REWARDS

If you start with a normal, healthy dog and give him time, patience and some carefully executed lessons, you will reap the rewards of that training for the life of the dog. And what a life it will be! The two of you will find immeasurable pleasure in the companionship you have built together with love, respect and understanding.

Training a puppy aged 10 to 16 weeks (20 weeks at the most) is like working with a dry sponge in a pool of water. The pup soaks up whatever you show him and constantly looks for more things to do and learn. At this early age, his body is not yet producing hormones, and therein lies the reason for such a high rate of success. Without hormones, he is focused on his owners and not particularly interested in investigating other places, dogs, people, etc. You are his leader: his provider of food, water, shelter and security. He latches onto you and wants to stay close. He will usually follow you from room to room, will not let you out of his sight when you are outdoors with him and will respond in like manner to the people and animals you encounter. If you greet a friend warmly, he will be willing to greet the person as well. If, however, you are hesitant or anxious about the approach of a stranger, he will respond to that person accordingly.

Once the puppy begins to produce hormones, his natural curiosity emerges and he begins to investigate the world around him. It is at this time when you may notice that the untrained dog begins to wander away from you and even ignore your commands to stay close. When this behavior becomes a problem, the owner has two choices: get rid of the dog or

PARENTAL GUIDANCE

Training a dog is a life experience. Many parents admit that much of what they know about raising children they learned from caring for their dogs. Dogs respond to love, fairness and guidance, just as children do. Become a good dog owner and you may become an even better parent.

train him. It is strongly urged that you choose the latter option.

There usually will be classes within a reasonable distance from your home, but you also do a lot to train your dog yourself. Sometimes there are classes available but the tuition is too

All dogs welcome structure in their routines and environments. Your Lhasa looks to you to provide this needed consistency, upon which his whole education will be based.

costly. Whatever the circumstances, the solution to training your Lhasa without formal obedience classes lies within the pages of this book. This chapter is devoted to helping you train your Lhasa Apso at home. If the recommended procedures are followed faithfully, you may

expect positive results that will prove rewarding to both you and your dog.

Whether your new charge is a puppy or a mature adult, the methods of teaching and the techniques we use in training basic behaviors are the same. After all, no dog, whether puppy or adult, likes harsh or inhumane methods. All creatures, however, respond favorably to gentle motivational methods and sincere praise and encouragement. Now let us get started.

HOUSEBREAKING

You can train a puppy to relieve himself wherever you choose, but this must be somewhere suitable. You should bear in mind from the outset that when your puppy is old enough to go out in public places, any canine deposits must be removed at once. You will always have to carry with you a small plastic bag or "poop-scoop."

Outdoor training includes such surfaces as grass, dirt and cement. Indoor training usually means training your dog to newspaper. When deciding on the surface and location that you will want your Lhasa Apso to use, be sure it is going to be permanent. Training your dog to grass and then changing your mind two months later is extremely difficult for both dog and owner.

Next, choose the command you will use each and every time

MEALTIME

Mealtime should be a peaceful time for your puppy. Do not put his food and water bowls in a high-traffic area in the house. For example, give him his own little corner of the kitchen where he can eat undisturbed and where he will not be underfoot. Do not allow small children or other family members to disturb the pup when he is eating.

THE CLEAN LIFE

By providing sleeping and resting quarters that fit the dog, and offering frequent opportunities to relieve himself outside his quarters, the puppy quickly learns that the outdoors is the place to go when he needs to urinate or defecate. It also reinforces his innate desire to keep his sleeping quarters clean. This, in turn, helps develop the muscle control that will eventually produce a dog with clean living habits.

you want your puppy to void. "Go hurry up" and "Potty" are examples of commands commonly used by dog owners.

Get in the habit of giving the puppy your chosen relief command before you take him out. That way, when he becomes an adult, you will be able to determine if he wants to go out when you ask him. A confirmation will be signs of interest, such as wagging his tail, watching you intently, going to the door, etc.

PUPPY'S NEEDS
The puppy needs to relieve himself after play periods, after each meal, after he has been sleeping and any time he indicates that he is looking for a place to urinate or defecate. The urinary and intestinal tract muscles of very young puppies are not fully developed. There-

Male dogs lift their legs around the borders of the yard, but usually will not make piddle stains in the center of your lawn.

HONOR AND OBEY

Dogs are the most honorable animals in existence. They consider another species (humans) as their own. They interface with you. You are their leader. Puppies perceive children to be on their level; their actions around small children are different from their behavior around their adult masters.

HOUSING

Since the types of housing and control you provide for your puppy have a direct relationship on the success of house-training, we consider the various aspects of both before we begin training.

Bringing a new puppy home and turning him loose in your house can be compared to turning a child loose in a sports arena and telling the child that the place is all his! The sheer enormity of the place would be too much for him to handle. Instead, offer the puppy clearly defined areas where he can play, sleep, eat and live. A room of the house where the family gathers is the most obvious choice. Puppies are social animals and need to feel a part of the pack right from the start. Hearing your voice, watching you while you are doing things and smelling you nearby are all positive reinforcers that he is now a member of your pack. Usually a family room, the kitchen or a nearby adjoining breakfast area is ideal for providing safety and security for both puppy and owner.

Within that room, there should be a smaller area that the puppy can call his own. A wire or fiberglass dog crate, from which he can view the activities of his new family, will be fine. The size of the crate is the key factor here. The area must be large enough for the puppy to lie down and stretch out as well as stand up without

fore, like human babies, puppies need to relieve themselves frequently.

Take your puppy out often—every hour for a 12-week-old, for example, and always immediately after sleeping and eating. The older the puppy, the less often he will need to relieve himself. Finally, as a mature healthy adult, he will require only three to five relief trips per day.

A well-trained Lhasa Apso is a wonderful combination of physical beauty and polite behavior.

HOW MANY TIMES A DAY?

AGE	RELIEF TRIPS
To 14 weeks	10
14–22 weeks	8
22–32 weeks	6
Adulthood	4
(dog stops growing)	

These are estimates, of course, but they are a guide to the *minimum* number of opportunities a dog should have each day to relieve himself.

rubbing his head on the top, yet small enough so that he cannot relieve himself at one end and sleep at the other without coming into contact with his droppings.

Dogs are, by nature, clean animals and will not remain close to their relief areas unless forced to do so. In those cases, they then become dirty dogs and usually remain that way for life.

The designated area should include clean bedding and a toy. Water must always be available, in a non-spill container, though

Your Apso should have a place to call his own that is both comfortable and conducive to housebreaking. A wire crate with bedding is all that is needed.

you should monitor your pup's water intake during house-breaking.

CONTROL

By *control*, we mean helping the puppy to create a lifestyle pattern that will be compatible to that of his human pack (*you!*). Just as we guide little children to learn our way of life, we must show the puppy when it is time to play, eat, sleep, exercise and even entertain himself.

PAPER CAPER

Never line your pup's sleeping area with newspaper. Puppy litters are usually raised on newspaper and, once in your home, the puppy will immediately associate newspaper with voiding. Never put newspaper on any floor while house-training, as this will only confuse the puppy. Finally, restrict water intake after evening meals. Offer a few licks at a time—never let a young puppy gulp water after meals; gulping water is not good for adult dogs, either.

Your puppy should always sleep in his crate. He should also learn that, during times of household confusion and excessive human activity such as at breakfast when family members are preparing for the day, he can play by himself in relative safety and comfort in his designated area. Each time you leave the puppy alone, he should understand exactly where he is to stay. Puppies are chewers. They cannot tell the difference between things like lamp cords, television wires, shoes, table legs, etc. Chewing into a television wire, for example, can be fatal to the puppy, while a shorted wire can start a fire in the house.

If the puppy chews on the arm of the chair when he is alone, you will probably discipline him angrily when you get home. Thus, he makes the association that your coming home means he is going to be punished. (He will not remember chewing the chair and is incapable of making the association of the discipline with his naughty deed.)

Times of excitement, such as family parties, visits, etc., can be fun for the puppy, providing he can view the activities from the security of his designated area. He is not underfoot and he is not being fed all sorts of tidbits that will probably cause him stomach distress, yet he still feels a part of the fun.

CANINE DEVELOPMENT SCHEDULE

It is important to understand how and at what age a puppy develops into adulthood. If you are a puppy owner, consult the following Canine Development Schedule to determine the stage of development your puppy is currently experiencing. This knowledge will help you as you work with the puppy in the weeks and months ahead.

Period	Age	Characteristics
FIRST TO THIRD	BIRTH TO SEVEN WEEKS	Puppy needs food, sleep and warmth, and responds to simple and gentle touching. Needs mother for security and disciplining. Needs littermates for learning and interacting with other dogs. Pup learns to function within a pack and learns pack order of dominance. Begin socializing pup with adults and children for short periods. Pup begins to become aware of his environment.
FOURTH	EIGHT TO TWELVE WEEKS	Brain is fully developed. Needs socializing with outside world. Remove from mother and littermates. Needs to change from canine pack to human pack. Human dominance necessary. Fear period occurs between 8 and 12 weeks. Avoid fright and pain.
FIFTH	THIRTEEN TO SIXTEEN WEEKS	Training and formal obedience should begin. Less association with other dogs, more with people, places, situations. Period will pass easily if you remember this is pup's change-to-adolescence time. Be firm and fair. Flight instinct prominent. Permissiveness and over-disciplining can do permanent damage. Praise for good behavior.
JUVENILE	FOUR TO EIGHT MONTHS	Another fear period about 7 to 8 months of age. It passes quickly, but be cautious of fright and pain. Sexual maturity reached. Dominant traits established. Dog should understand sit, down, come and stay by now.

NOTE: THESE ARE APPROXIMATE TIME FRAMES. ALLOW FOR INDIVIDUAL DIFFERENCES IN PUPPIES.

SCHEDULE

A puppy should be taken to his relief area each time he is released from his designated area, after meals, after play sessions, when he first awakens in the morning (at age 12 weeks, this can mean 5 a.m.!). The puppy will indicate that he's ready "to go" by circling or sniffing busily—do not misinterpret these signs. For a very young puppy, a routine of taking him out every hour is necessary. As the puppy grows, he will be able to wait for longer periods of time.

Keep trips to his relief area short. Stay no more than five or six minutes and then return to the house. If he goes during that time, praise him lavishly and take him indoors immediately. If

THE SUCCESS METHOD
6 Steps to Successful Crate Training

Success that comes by luck is usually short-lived. Success that comes by well-thought-out proven methods is often more easily achieved and permanent. This is the Success Method. It is designed to give you, the puppy owner, a simple yet proven way to help your puppy develop clean living habits and a feeling of security in his new environment.

1 Tell the puppy "Crate time!" and place him in the crate with a small treat (a piece of cheese or half of a biscuit). Let him stay in the crate for five minutes while you are in the same room. Then release him and praise lavishly. Never release him when he is fussing. Wait until he is quiet before you let him out.

2 Repeat Step 1 several times a day.

3 The next day, place the puppy in the crate as before. Let him stay there for ten minutes. Do this several times.

4 Continue building time in five-minute increments until the puppy stays in his crate for 30 minutes with you in the room. Always take him to his relief area after prolonged periods in his crate.

5 Now go back to Step 1 and let the puppy stay in his crate for five minutes, this time while you are out of the room.

6 Once again, build crate time in five-minute increments with you out of the room. When the puppy will stay willingly in his crate (he may even fall asleep!) for 30 minutes with you out of the room, he will be ready to stay in it for several hours at a time.

HOUSE-TRAINING TIP

Most of all, be consistent. Always take your dog to the same location, always use the same command and always have the dog on lead when he is in his relief area, unless a fenced-in yard is available.

By following the Success Method, your puppy will be completely housebroken by the time his muscle and brain development reach maturity. Keep in mind that small breeds usually mature faster than large breeds, but all puppies should be trained by six months of age.

outdoors means it is time to relieve himself, not play. Once trained, he will be able to play indoors and out and still differentiate between the times for play versus the times for relief.

Help him develop regular hours for naps, being alone, playing by himself and just resting, all in his crate. Encourage him to entertain himself while you are busy with your activities. Let him learn that having you near is comforting, but it is not your main purpose in life to provide him with undivided attention. Each time you put a puppy in his

he does not, but he has an accident when you go back indoors, pick him up immediately, say "No! No!" and return to his relief area. Wait a few minutes, then return to the house again. Never hit a puppy or put his face in urine or excrement when he has an accident!

Once indoors, put the puppy in his crate until you have had time to clean up his accident. Then release him to the family area and watch him more closely than before. Chances are, his accident was a result of your not picking up his signal or waiting too long before offering him the opportunity to relieve himself. Never hold a grudge against the puppy for accidents.

Let the puppy learn that going

A well-trained Lhasa makes a beautiful, polite and enjoyable companion with whom you'll delight in sharing your home.

own area, use the same command, whatever suits best. Soon, he will run to his crate when he hears you say those words.

Crate training provides safety for you, the puppy and the home. It also provides the puppy with a feeling of security, and that helps the puppy achieve self-confidence and clean habits. Remember that one of the primary ingredients in house-training your puppy is control. Regardless of your lifestyle, there will always be occasions when you will need to

Always clean up after your dog, even if it is in your own yard.

have a place where your dog can stay and be happy and safe. Crate training is the answer for now and in the future.

In conclusion, a few key elements are really all you need for a successful house-training method—consistency, frequency, praise, control and supervision. By following these procedures with a normal, healthy puppy, you and the puppy will soon be past the stage of accidents and ready to move on to a clean and rewarding life together.

TAKE THE LEAD

Do not carry your dog to his relief area. Lead him there on a leash or, better yet, encourage him to follow you to the spot. If you start carrying him to his spot, you might end up doing this routine forever and your dog will have the satisfaction of having trained *you*.

ROLES OF DISCIPLINE, REWARD AND PUNISHMENT

Discipline, training one to act in accordance with rules, brings order to life. It is as simple as that. Without discipline, particularly in a group society, chaos reigns supreme and the group will eventually perish. Humans and canines are social animals and need some form of discipline in order to function effectively. They must procure food, reproduce to keep the species going and protect their home base and their young. If there were no discipline in the lives of social animals, they would eventually die from starvation and/or predation by other stronger animals. In the case of domestic canines, dogs need discipline in their lives in order to understand how their pack (you and other family members) functions and how they must act in order to survive.

A large humane society in a highly populated area recently surveyed dog owners regarding their satisfaction with their relationships with their dogs. People who had trained their dogs were 75% more satisfied with their pets than those who had never trained their dogs.

Dr. Edward Thorndike, a well-known psychologist, established *Thorndike's Theory of Learning*, which states that a behavior that results in a pleasant event tends to be repeated. Likewise, a behavior that results in an unpleasant event tends not to be repeated. It is this theory on which training methods are based today. For example, if you manipulate a dog to perform a specific behavior and reward him for doing it, he is likely to do it again because he enjoyed the end result.

Occasionally, punishment, a penalty inflicted for an offense, is necessary. The best type of punishment often comes from an outside source. For example, a child is told not to touch the stove because he may get burned. He disobeys and touches the stove. In doing so, he receives a burn. From that time on, he respects the heat of the stove and avoids contact with it. Therefore, a behavior that results in an unpleasant event tends not to be repeated.

A good example of a dog learning the hard way is the dog who chases the house cat. He is told many times to leave the cat alone, yet he persists in teasing the cat. Then, one day he begins chasing the cat but the cat turns and swipes a claw across the dog's face, leaving him with a painful gash on his nose. The final result is that the dog stops chasing the cat.

TRAINING EQUIPMENT

COLLAR AND LEAD
For a Lhasa Apso, the collar and lead that you use for training must be one with which you are easily able to work, not too heavy for the dog and perfectly safe.

TREATS
Have a bag of treats on hand. Something nutritious and easy to swallow works best. Use a soft treat,

PLAN TO PLAY

The puppy should also have regular play and exercise sessions when he is with you or a family member. Exercise for a very young puppy can consist of a short walk around the house or yard. Playing can include fetching games with a ball or a special toy. (All puppies teethe and need soft things upon which to chew.) Remember to restrict play periods to indoors within his living area (the family room, for example) until he is completely house-trained.

Lead training the Lhasa Apso requires little more than the equipment and the time and effort to introduce your dog to the exercise.

a chunk of cheese or a piece of cooked chicken rather than a dry biscuit. By the time the dog gets done chewing a dry treat, he will forget why he is being rewarded in the first place! By the way, using food rewards will not teach a dog to beg at the table—the only way to teach a dog to beg at the table is to give him food from the table. In training, rewarding the dog with a food treat will help him associate praise and the treats with learning new behaviors that obviously please his owner.

TRAINING BEGINS: ASK THE DOG A QUESTION

In order to teach your dog anything, you must first get his attention. After all, he cannot

PRACTICE MAKES PERFECT!

- Have training lessons with your dog every day in several short segments—three to five times a day for a few minutes at a time is ideal.
- Do not have long practice sessions. The dog will become easily bored.
- Never practice when you are tired, ill, worried or in an otherwise negative mood. This will transmit to the dog and may have an adverse effect on his performance.

  Think fun, short and above all *positive*! End each session on a high note, rather than a failed exercise, and make sure to give a lot of praise. Enjoy the training and help your dog enjoy it, too.

learn anything if he is looking away from you with his mind on something else.

To get his attention, ask him "School?" and immediately walk over to him and give him a treat as you tell him "Good dog." Wait a minute or two and repeat the routine, this time with a treat in your hand as you approach within a foot of the dog. Do not go directly to him, but stop about a foot short of him and hold out the treat as you ask "School?" He will see you approaching with a treat in your hand and most

words, he learns that "school" means doing fun things with you that result in treats and positive attention for him.

Remember that the dog does not understand your verbal language, he only recognizes sounds. Your question translates to a series of sounds for him, and those sounds become the signal to go to you and pay attention; if he does, he will get to interact with you plus receive treats and praise.

THE BASIC COMMANDS

TEACHING SIT

Now that you have the dog's attention, attach his lead and hold it in your left hand and a food treat in your right. Place your food hand at the dog's nose

Dogs are easily motivated in training by food rewards.

likely begin walking toward you. As you meet, give him the treat and praise again.

The third time, ask the question, have a treat in your hand and walk only a short distance toward the dog so that he must walk almost all the way to you. As he reaches you, give him the treat and praise again.

By this time, the dog will probably be getting the idea that if he pays attention to you, especially when you ask that question, it will pay off in treats and fun activities for him. In other

LANGUAGE BARRIER

Dogs do not understand our language and have to rely on tone of voice more than just words or sound. They can be trained to react to a certain sound, at a certain volume. If you say "No, Oliver" in a very soft, pleasant voice, it will not have the same meaning as "No, Oliver!!" when you say it loudly. You should never use the dog's name during a reprimand, just the command "No! " You never want the dog to associate his name with a negative experience or reprimand.

and let him lick the treat but not take it from you. Say "Sit" and slowly raise your food hand from in front of the dog's nose up over his head so that he is looking at the ceiling. As he bends his head upward, he will have to bend his knees to maintain his balance. As he bends his knees, he will assume a sit position. At that point, release the food treat and praise lavishly with comments such as "Good dog! Good sit!" Remember to always praise

Don't overdo it with food rewards—a puppy or small dog has a relatively low daily calorie requirement and treats can add up quickly.

enthusiastically, because dogs relish verbal praise from their owners and feel so proud of themselves whenever they accomplish a behavior.

You will not use food forever in getting the dog to obey your commands. Food is only used to teach new behaviors, and once the dog knows what you want when you give a specific command, you will wean him off the food treats

but still maintain the verbal praise. After all, you will always have your voice with you, and there will be many times when you have no food rewards but expect the dog to obey.

TEACHING DOWN

Teaching the down exercise is easy when you understand how the dog perceives the down position, and it is very difficult when you do not. Dogs perceive the down position as a submissive one; therefore, teaching the down exercise using a forceful method can sometimes make the dog develop such a fear of the down that he either runs away when you say "Down" or he attempts to snap at the person who tries to force him down.

Have the dog sit close alongside your left leg, facing in the same direction as you are. Hold the lead in your left hand and a food treat in your right. Now place your left hand lightly on the top of the dog's shoulders where they meet above the spinal cord. Do not push down on the dog's shoulders; simply rest your left hand there so you can guide the dog to lie down close to your left leg rather than to swing away from your side when he drops.

Teaching basic commands can be done with a combination of verbal commands and hand signals.

Now place the food hand at the dog's nose, say "Down" very softly (almost a whisper) and slowly lower the food hand to the dog's front feet. When the food hand reaches the floor, begin moving it forward along the floor in front of the dog. Keep talking softly to the dog, saying things like, "Do you want this treat? You can do this, good dog." Your reassuring tone of voice will help calm the dog as he tries to follow the food hand in order to get the treat.

When the dog's elbows touch the floor, release the food and praise softly. Try to get the dog to maintain that down position for several seconds before you let him sit up again. The goal here is to get the dog to settle down

DOUBLE JEOPARDY

A dog in jeopardy never lies down. He stays alert on his feet because instinct tells him that he may have to run away or fight for his survival. Therefore, if a dog feels threatened or anxious, he will not lie down. Consequently, it is important to keep the dog calm and relaxed as he learns the down exercise.

and not feel threatened in the down position.

TEACHING STAY

It is easy to teach the dog to stay in either a sit or a down position. Again, we use food and praise during the teaching process as we help the dog to understand

FAMILY TIES

If you have other pets in the home and/or interact often with the pets of friends and other family members, your pup will respond to those pets in much the same manner as you do. It is only when you show fear of or resentment toward another animal that he will act fearful or unfriendly.

exactly what it is that we are expecting him to do.

To teach the sit/stay, start with the dog sitting on your left side as before and hold the lead in your left hand. Have a food treat in your right hand and place your food hand at the dog's nose. Say "Stay" and step out on your right foot to stand directly in front of the dog, toe to toe, as he licks and nibbles the treat. Be sure to keep his head facing upward to maintain the sit position. Count to five and then swing around to stand next to the dog again with him on your left. As soon as you get back to the original position, release the food and praise lavishly.

To teach the down/stay, do the

down as previously described. As soon as the dog lies down, say "Stay" and step out on your right foot just as you did in the sit/stay. Count to five and then return to stand beside the dog with him on your left side. Release the treat and praise as always.

Within a week or ten days, you can begin to add a bit of distance between you and your dog when you leave him. When you do, use your left hand open with the palm facing the dog as a stay signal, much the same as the hand signal a police officer uses to stop traffic at an intersection. Hold the food treat in your right hand as before, but this time the food is not touching the dog's nose. He will watch the food hand and quickly learn that he is going to get that treat as soon as you return to his side.

When you can stand 3 feet away from your dog for 30 seconds, you can then begin building time and distance in both stays. Eventually, the dog can be expected to remain in the stay position for prolonged periods of time until you return to him or call him to you. Always praise lavishly when he stays.

TEACHING COME

If you make teaching "come" a fun experience, you should never have a student that does not love the game or that fails to come when called. The secret, it seems, is never to teach the word "come."

At times when an owner most wants his dog to come when called, the owner is likely upset or anxious and he allows these feelings to come through in the tone of his voice when he calls his dog. Hearing that desperation in his owner's voice, the dog fears the results of going to him and therefore either disobeys outright or runs in the opposite direction. The secret, therefore, is to teach the dog a game and, when you want him to come to you, simply play the game. It is practically a no-fail solution!

To begin, have several members of your family take a few food treats and each go into a different room in the house. Take turns calling the dog, and each person should celebrate the dog's finding him with a treat and lots of happy praise. When a person calls the dog, he is actually inviting the dog to find him and get a

"COME" . . . BACK

Never call your dog to come to you for a correction or scold him when he reaches you. That is the quickest way to turn a come command into "Go away fast!" Dogs think only in the present tense, and your dog will connect the scolding with coming to you, not with the misbehavior of a few moments earlier.

"WHERE ARE YOU?"

When calling the dog, do not say "Come." Say things like, "Rover, where are you? See if you can find me! I have a biscuit for you!" Keep up a constant line of chatter with coaxing sounds and frequent questions such as, "Where are you?" The dog will learn to follow the sound of your voice to locate you and receive his reward.

treat as a reward for "winning."

A few turns of the "Where are you?" game and the dog will figure out that everyone is playing the game and that each person has a big celebration awaiting his success at locating them. Once he learns to love the game, simply calling out "Where are you?" will bring him running from wherever he is when he hears that all-important question.

The come command is recognized as one of the most important things to teach a dog, but there are trainers who work with thousands of dogs and never teach the actual word "come." Yet these dogs will race to respond to a person who uses the dog's name followed by "Where are you?" For example, a woman has a 12-year-old companion dog who went blind, but who never fails to locate her owner when asked, "Where are you?"

Children particularly love to play this game with their dogs. Children can hide in smaller places like a shower or bathtub, behind a bed or under a table. The dog needs to work a little bit harder to find these hiding places, but, when he does, he loves to celebrate with a treat and a tussle with a favorite youngster.

TEACHING HEEL

Heeling means that the dog walks beside the owner without pulling. It takes time and patience on the owner's part to succeed at teaching the dog that he (the owner) will not proceed unless the dog is walking calmly beside him. Pulling out ahead on the lead is definitely not acceptable.

Begin with holding the lead in your left hand as the dog sits beside your left leg. Move the loop end of the lead to your right hand but keep your left hand short on the lead so it keeps the dog in close next to you.

Say "Heel" and step forward on your left foot. Keep the dog close to you and take three steps. Stop and have the dog sit next to you in what we now call the heel position. Praise verbally, but do not touch the dog. Hesitate a moment and begin again with "Heel," taking three steps and stopping, at which point the dog is told to sit again.

Your goal here is to have the dog walk those three steps without pulling on the lead. When he

All dogs must be trained to heel so that they will behave politely during everyday walks.

will walk calmly beside you for three steps without pulling, increase the number of steps you take to five. When he will walk politely beside you while you take five steps, you can increase the length of your walk to ten steps. Keep increasing the length of your stroll until the dog will walk quietly beside you without pulling as long as you want him to heel. When you stop heeling, indicate to the dog that the exercise is over by verbally praising as you pet him and say "OK, good dog." The "OK" is used as a release word, meaning that the exercise is finished and the dog is free to relax.

If you are dealing with a dog who insists on pulling you around, simply "put on your

TUG OF WALK?

If you begin teaching the heel by taking walks and letting the dog pull you along, he misinterprets this action as an acceptable form of taking a walk. When you pull back on the lead to counteract his pulling, he reads that tug as a signal to pull even harder!

brakes" and stand your ground until the dog realizes that the two of you are not going anywhere until he is beside you and moving at your pace, not his. It may take some time just standing there to convince the dog that you are the leader and you will be the one to decide on the direction and speed of your travel.

Each time the dog looks up at you or slows down to give a slack lead between the two of you, quietly praise him and say, "Good heel. Good dog." Eventually, the dog will begin to respond and within a few days he will be walking politely beside you without pulling on the lead. At first, the training

A BORN PRODIGY

Occasionally, a dog and owner who have not attended formal classes have been able to earn entry-level titles by obtaining competition rules and regulations from the hosting club and practicing on their own to a degree of perfection. Obtaining the higher level titles, however, almost always requires extensive training under the tutelage of experienced instructors. In addition, the more difficult levels require more specialized equipment whereas the lower levels do not.

sessions should be kept short and very positive; soon the dog will be able to walk nicely with you for increasingly longer distances. Remember also to give the dog free time and the opportunity to run and play when you are done with heel practice.

WEANING OFF FOOD IN TRAINING

Food is used in training new behaviors. Once the dog understands what behavior goes with a specific command, it is time to start weaning him off the food treats. At first, give a treat after each exercise. Then, start to give a treat only after every other exercise. Mix up the times when you offer a food reward and the times when you offer only praise so that the dog will never know when he is going to receive both food and praise and when he is going to receive only praise. This is called a variable-ratio reward system and it proves successful because there is always the chance that the owner will produce a treat, so the dog never stops trying for that reward. No matter what, *always* give verbal praise.

OBEDIENCE CLASSES

It is a good idea to enroll in an obedience class if one is available in your area. If yours is a show dog, handling classes would be more appropriate. Many areas

OBEDIENCE SCHOOL

A basic obedience beginner's class usually lasts for six to eight weeks. Dog and owner attend an hour-long lesson once a week and practice for a few minutes, several times a day, each day at home. If done properly, the whole procedure will result in a well-mannered dog and an owner who delights in living with a pet that is eager to please and enjoys doing things with his owner.

have dog clubs that offer basic obedience training as well as preparatory classes for obedience competition. There are also local dog trainers who offer similar classes.

At obedience trials, dogs can earn titles at various levels of competition. The beginning levels of competition include basic behaviors such as sit, down, heel, etc. The more advanced levels of competition include jumping, retrieving, scent discrimination and signal work. The advanced levels require a dog and owner to put a lot of time and effort into their training, and the titles that can be earned at these levels of competition are very prestigious.

OTHER ACTIVITIES FOR LIFE

Whether a dog is trained in the structured environment of a class or alone with his owner at home there are many activities that can bring fun and rewards to both owner and dog once they have mastered basic control.

Teaching the dog to help out around the home or in the yard provides great satisfaction to both dog and owner. In addition, the dog's help makes life a little easier for his owner and raises the dog's stature as a valued companion to his family. It helps give the dog a purpose by occupying his mind and providing an outlet for his energy.

Hiking is an exciting and healthy activity that the dog can be taught without assistance from more than his owner. The exercise of walking and climbing is good for man and dog alike, and the bond that they develop together is priceless.

If you are interested in participating in organized competition with your Lhasa Apso, there are activities other than obedience in which you and your dog can become involved. Agility is a popular and fun sport where dogs run through an obstacle course that includes various jumps, tunnels and other exercises to test the dog's speed and coordination. The owners run through the course beside their dogs to give commands and to guide them through the course. Although competitive, the focus is on fun—it's fun to do, fun to watch, and great exercise.

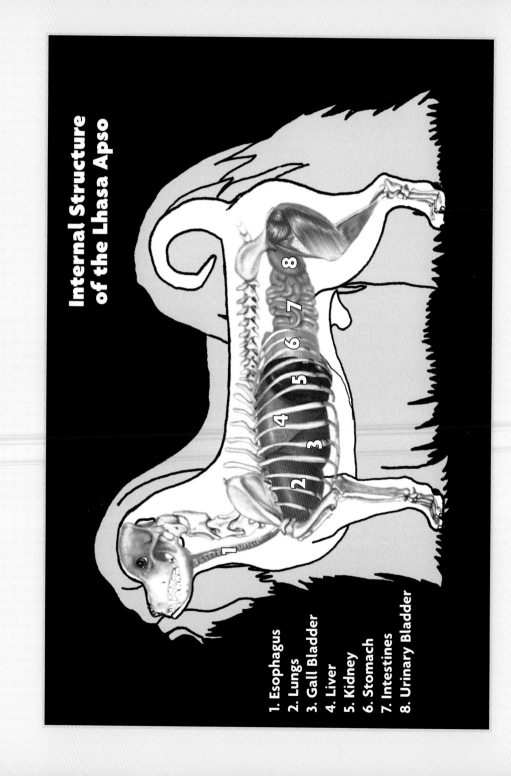

Internal Structure
of the Lhasa Apso

1. Esophagus
2. Lungs
3. Gall Bladder
4. Liver
5. Kidney
6. Stomach
7. Intestines
8. Urinary Bladder

Health Care of Your
LHASA APSO

Dogs suffer from many of the same physical illnesses as people. Since people usually know more about human diseases than canine maladies, many of the terms used in this chapter will be familiar but not necessarily those used by veterinarians. We will use the term *x-ray*, instead of the more acceptable term *radiograph*. We will also use the familiar term *symptoms* even though dogs don't have symptoms, which are verbal descriptions of the patient's feelings, dogs have *clinical signs*. Since dogs can't speak, we have to look for clinical signs...but we still use the term *symptoms* in this book.

As a general rule, medicine is *practiced*. That term is not arbitrary. Medicine is a constantly changing art as we learn more and more about genetics, electronic aids (like CAT scans and MRIs) and daily laboratory advances. There are many dog maladies, like hip dysplasia, which are not universally treated in the same manner. For example, some veterinarians opt for surgery more often than others do.

SELECTING A QUALIFIED VET
Your selection of a veterinarian should be based not only upon his personality and ability with small dogs but also upon his convenience to your home. You want a vet who is close because you might have emergencies or need to make multiple visits for treatments. You want a vet who has services that you might require such as a boarding kennel and grooming facilities, as well as sophisticated pet supplies and a good reputation for ability and responsiveness. There is nothing more frustrating than having to wait a day or more to get a response from your veterinarian.

All veterinarians are licensed and their diplomas and/or certificates should be displayed in their

Before you buy your Lhasa Apso, meet and interview the veterinarians in your area. Take everything into consideration; discuss background, specialties, fees, emergency policy, etc.

Breakdown of Veterinary Income by Category

2%	Dentistry
4%	Radiology
12%	Surgery
15%	Vaccinations
19%	Laboratory
23%	Examinations
25%	Medicines

A typical vet's income, categorized according to services performed. This survey dealt with small-animal (pets) practices.

waiting rooms. There are, however, many veterinary specialties that usually require further studies and internships. There are specialists in heart problems (veterinary cardiologists), skin problems (veterinary dermatologists), teeth and gum problems (veterinary dentists), eye problems (veterinary ophthalmologists) and x-rays (veterinary radiologists), and vets who have specialties in bones, muscles or certain organs. Most veterinarians do routine surgery such as neutering, stitching up wounds and docking tails for those breeds in which such is required for show purposes. When the problem affecting your dog is serious, it is not unusual or impudent to get another medical opinion, although it is courteous to advise the vets concerned about this. You might also want to compare costs among several

veterinarians. Sophisticated health care and veterinary services can be very costly. Don't be bashful about discussing these costs with your veterinarian or his staff. It is not infrequent that important decisions are based upon financial considerations.

PREVENTATIVE MEDICINE

It is much easier, less costly and more effective to practice preventative medicine than to fight bouts of illness and disease. Properly bred puppies come from parents that were selected based upon their genetic-disease profiles. Their dam should have been vaccinated, free of all internal and external parasites and properly nourished. For these reasons, it is important to learn as much about the dam's health as possible. The dam can pass on disease resistance to her puppies, which can last for eight to ten weeks, but she

WORMING PROGRAM

Caring for the puppy starts before the puppy is born by keeping the dam healthy and well-nourished. Most puppies have worms, even if they are not evident, so a worming program is essential. The worms continually shed eggs except during their dormant stage, when they just rest in the tissues of the puppy. During this stage they are not evident during a routine examination.

First Aid at a Glance

Burns
Place the affected area under cool water; use ice if only a small area is burnt.

Bee stings/Insect bites
Apply ice to relieve swelling; antihistamine dosed properly.

Animal bites
Clean any bleeding area; apply pressure until bleeding subsides; go to the vet.

Spider bites
Use cold compress and a pressurized pack to inhibit venom's spreading.

Antifreeze poisoning
Immediately induce vomiting by using hydrogen peroxide.

Fish hooks
Removal best handled by vet; hook must be cut in order to remove.

Snake bites
Pack ice around bite; contact vet quickly; identify snake for proper antivenin.

Car accident
Move dog from roadway with blanket; seek veterinary aid.

Shock
Calm the dog, keep him warm; seek immediate veterinary help.

Nosebleed
Apply cold compress to the nose; apply pressure to any visible abrasion.

Bleeding
Apply pressure above the area; treat wound by applying a cotton pack.

Heat stroke
Submerge dog in cold bath; cool down with fresh air and water; go to the vet.

Frostbite/Hypothermia
Warm the dog with a warm bath, electric blankets or hot water bottles.

Abrasions
Clean the wound and wash out thoroughly with fresh water; apply antiseptic.

 Remember: an injured dog may attempt to bite a helping hand from fear and confusion. Always muzzle the dog before trying to offer assistance.

can also pass on parasites and many infections.

WEANING TO BRINGING PUP HOME
Puppies should be weaned by the time they are about two months old. A puppy that remains for *at least* eight weeks with his mother and littermates usually adapts better to other dogs and people later in his life. Owners usually have their new puppies examined by the veterinarian immediately, which is a good idea.

The puppy will have his teeth examined and have his skeletal conformation and general health checked prior to certification by the veterinarian. Puppies in certain breeds have problems with their kneecaps, cataracts and other eye problems, heart murmurs and undescended testicles. Your vet might also have training in temperament evaluation. At the first visit, the vet will set up a schedule for the pup's vaccination program.

VACCINATION SCHEDULING
Most vaccinations are given by injection and should only be done by a veterinarian. Both he and you should keep a record of the date of the injection, the identification of the vaccine and the amount given. Some vets give a first vaccination at six weeks, but most dog breeders prefer the course not to commence until about eight weeks because of negating any

---

NEUTERING/SPAYING

Male dogs are castrated. The operation removes both testicles and requires that the dog be anesthetized. Recovery takes about one week. Females are spayed; in this operation, the uterus (womb) and both of the ovaries are removed. This is major surgery, also carried out under general anesthesia, and it usually takes a bitch two weeks to recover.

---

antibodies passed on by the dam. The vaccination scheduling is usually based on a two- to four-week cycle. You must take your vet's advice as to when to vaccinate as this may differ according to the vaccine used.

Most vaccinations immunize your puppy against viruses. The usual vaccines contain immunizing doses of several different viruses such as distemper, parvovirus, parainfluenza and hepatitis. There are other vaccines available when the puppy is at risk. You should rely upon professional advice. This is especially true for the booster-shot program. Most vaccination programs require a booster when the puppy is a year old and once a year thereafter. In some cases, circumstances may require more frequent immunizations. Canine cough, more formally known as tracheobronchitis, is treated with a vaccine that is sprayed into the

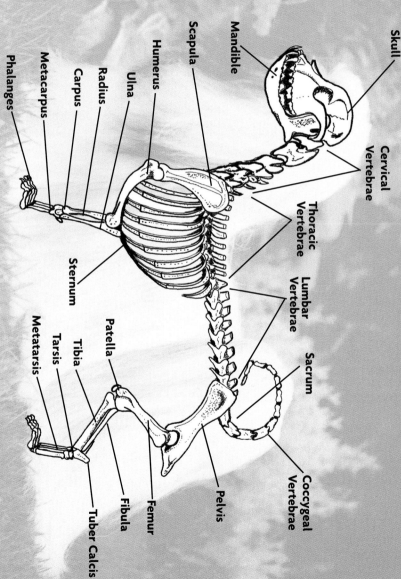

Lhasa Apso Skeletal Structure

Skull

Cervical Vertebrae

Mandible

Scapula

Humerus

Ulna

Radius

Carpus

Metacarpus

Phalanges

Thoracic Vertebrae

Lumbar Vertebrae

Sternum

Sacrum

Coccygeal Vertebrae

Metatarsis

Tarsis

Tibia

Patella

Fibula

Femur

Pelvis

Tuber Calcis

HEALTH AND VACCINATION SCHEDULE

AGE IN WEEKS:	3RD	6TH	8TH	10TH	12TH	14TH	16TH	20-24TH
Worm Control	✔	✔	✔	✔	✔	✔	✔	✔
Neutering								✔
Heartworm		✔						✔
Parvovirus		✔		✔		✔		✔
Distemper			✔		✔		✔	
Hepatitis			✔		✔		✔	
Leptospirosis		✔		✔		✔		
Parainfluenza		✔		✔		✔		
Dental Examination			✔					✔
Complete Physical			✔					✔
Temperament Testing			✔					
Coronavirus					✔			
Canine Cough		✔						
Hip Dysplasia							✔	
Rabies								✔

Vaccinations are not instantly effective. It takes about two weeks for the dog's immune system to develop antibodies. Most vaccinations require annual booster shots. Your vet should guide you in this regard.

dog's nostrils. Canine cough is usually included in routine vaccination, but this is often not as effective as the vaccines for other major diseases.

FIVE MONTHS TO ONE YEAR OF AGE
Unless you intend to breed or show your dog, neutering the puppy around six months of age is recommended. Discuss this with your veterinarian. Most professionals advise that you neuter (males) or spay (females) pet dogs, and responsible breeders will require this as part of their sales agreement for pet-quality

pups. Neutering/spaying has proven to be extremely beneficial to both male and female dogs. Besides eliminating the possibility of pregnancy and pyometra in bitches and testicular cancer in males, it greatly reduces the risk of breast cancer in bitches and prostate cancer in male dogs.

DOGS OLDER THAN ONE YEAR
Continue to visit the veterinarian at least once a year. There is no such disease as old age, but bodily functions do change with age. The eyes and ears are no longer as efficient. Liver, kidney and intestinal

functions often decline. Proper dietary changes, recommended by your veterinarian, can make life more pleasant for the aging Lhasa Apso and you.

SKIN PROBLEMS IN LHASA APSOS

Veterinarians are consulted by dog owners for skin problems more than any other group of diseases or maladies. Dogs' skin is almost as sensitive as human skin and both suffer from almost the same ailments (though the occurrence of acne in most dogs is rare!). For this reason, veterinarian dermatology has developed into a specialty practiced by many veterinarians.

VACCINE ALLERGIES

Vaccines do not work all the time. Sometimes dogs are allergic to them and many times the antibodies, which are supposed to be stimulated by the vaccine, just are not produced. You should keep your dog in the veterinary clinic for an hour after he is vaccinated to be sure there are no allergic reactions.

Disease	What is it?	What causes it?	Symptoms
Leptospirosis	Severe disease that affects the internal organs; can be spread to people.	A bacterium, which is often carried by rodents, that enters through mucous membranes and spreads quickly throughout the body.	Range from fever, vomiting and loss of appetite in less severe cases to shock, irreversible kidney damage and possibly death in most severe cases.
Rabies	Potentially deadly virus that infects warm-blooded mammals.	Bite from a carrier of the virus, mainly wild animals.	1st stage: dog exhibits change in behavior, fear. 2nd stage: dog's behavior becomes more aggressive. 3rd stage: loss of coordination, trouble with bodily functions.
Parvovirus	Highly contagious virus, potentially deadly.	Ingestion of the virus, which is usually spread through the feces of infected dogs.	Most common: severe diarrhea. Also vomiting, fatigue, lack of appetite.
Canine cough	Contagious respiratory infection.	Combination of types of bacteria and virus. Most common: *Bordetella bronchiseptica* bacteria and parainfluenza virus.	Chronic cough.
Distemper	Disease primarily affecting respiratory and nervous system.	Virus that is related to the human measles virus.	Mild symptoms such as fever, lack of appetite and mucus secretion progress to evidence of brain damage, "hard pad."
Hepatitis	Virus primarily affecting the liver.	Canine adenovirus type I (CAV-1). Enters system when dog breathes in particles.	Lesser symptoms include listlessness, diarrhea, vomiting. More severe symptoms include "blue-eye" (clumps of virus in eye).
Coronavirus	Virus resulting in digestive problems.	Virus is spread through infected dog's feces.	Stomach upset evidenced by lack of appetite, vomiting, diarrhea.

Since many skin problems have visual symptoms that are almost identical, it requires the skill of an experienced veterinary dermatologist to identify and cure many of the more severe skin disorders. Pet shops sell many treatments for skin problems, but most of the treatments are directed at symptoms and not the underlying problem(s). If your dog is suffering from a skin disorder, you should seek professional assistance as quickly as possible. As with all diseases, the earlier a problem is identified and treated, the more successful can be the cure.

HEREDITARY SKIN DISORDERS

Veterinary dermatologists are currently researching a number of skin disorders that are believed to have a hereditary basis. These inherited diseases are transmitted by both parents, who appear (phenotypically) normal but have a recessive gene for the disease, meaning that they carry, but are not affected by, the disease. These diseases pose serious problems to breeders because in some instances there are no methods of identifying carriers. Often the secondary diseases associated with these skin conditions are even more debilitating than the skin disorders themselves, including cancers and respiratory problems.

Among the hereditary skin disorders, for which the mode of

DENTAL HEALTH

A dental examination is in order when the dog is between six months and one year of age so that any permanent teeth that have erupted incorrectly can be corrected. Durable nylon and safe edible chews should be a part of your puppy's arsenal for good health, good teeth and pleasant breath. The vast majority of dogs three to four years old and older has diseases of the gums from lack of dental attention. Using the various types of dental chews can be very effective in controlling dental plaque.

inheritance is known, are cutaneous asthenia (Ehlers-Danlos syndrome), sebaceous adenitis, cyclic hematopoiesis, dermatomyositis, IgA deficiency, color dilution alopecia and nodular dermatofibrosis. All inherited diseases must be diagnosed and treated by a veterinary specialist.

PARASITE BITES

Many of us are allergic to insect bites. The bites itch, erupt and may even become infected. Dogs have the same reaction to fleas, ticks and/or mites. When an insect lands on you, you have the chance to whisk it away with your hand. Unfortunately, when your dog is bitten by a flea, tick or mite, he can only scratch it away or bite it. By the time the dog has been bitten, the parasite has done

In Korea, where the breed is very much appreciated, a veterinarian at the Samsung Toy Dog Kennel examines a Lhasa Apso.

some of its damage. It may also have laid eggs to cause further problems in the near future. The itching from parasite bites is probably due to the saliva injected into the site when the parasite sucks the dog's blood.

AUTO-IMMUNE SKIN CONDITIONS

Auto-immune skin conditions are commonly referred to as being allergic to yourself, while allergies are usually inflammatory reactions to an outside stimulus. Auto-immune diseases cause serious damage to the tissues that are involved. The best known auto-immune disease is lupus, which affects people as well as dogs. The symptoms are variable and may affect the kidneys, bones, blood chemistry and skin. It can be fatal to both dogs and humans, though it is not thought to be transmissible. It is usually successfully treated with cortisone, prednisone or similar corticosteroid, but extensive use of these drugs can have harmful side effects.

AIRBORNE ALLERGIES

Just as humans have hay fever, rose fever and other fevers from which they suffer during the pollinating season, many dogs suffer from the same allergies.

The portrait of good health. Responsible breeders only breed from dogs who have been screened for potential hereditary diseases. Do not purchase from a breeder who is not concerned about hereditary problems in his line.

When the pollen count is high, your dog might suffer, but don't expect him to sneeze and have a runny nose like a human would. Dogs react to pollen allergies the same way they react to fleas—they scratch and bite themselves.

Dogs, like humans, can be tested for allergens. Discuss the testing with your veterinary dermatologist.

FOOD PROBLEMS

FOOD ALLERGIES
Dogs can be allergic to many foods that are best-sellers and highly recommended by breeders and veterinarians. Changing the brand of food that you buy may

not eliminate the problem if the element to which the dog is allergic is contained in the new brand.

Recognizing a food allergy is difficult. Humans vomit or have rashes when they eat a food to which they are allergic. Dogs neither vomit nor (usually) develop a rash. They react in the same manner as they do to an airborne or flea allergy: they itch,

PROTEIN NEEDS

Your dog's protein needs are changeable. High activity level, stress, climate and other physical factors may require your dog to have more protein in his diet. Check with your veterinarian.

scratch and bite, thus making the diagnosis extremely difficult. While pollen allergies and parasite bites are usually seasonal, food allergies are year-round problems.

FOOD INTOLERANCE

Food intolerance is the inability of the dog to completely digest certain foods. For example, puppies that may have done very well on their mother's milk may not do well on cow's milk. The result of this food intolerance may be loose bowels, passing gas and stomach pains. These are the only obvious symptoms of food intolerance and that makes diagnosis difficult.

TREATING FOOD PROBLEMS

It is possible to handle food allergies and food intolerance yourself. Put your dog on a diet that he has never had. Obviously, if he has never eaten this new food, he can't yet have been allergic or intolerant of it. Start with a single ingredient that is not in the dog's diet at the present time. Ingredients like chopped beef or chicken are common in dog's diets, so try something else like fish, rabbit, lamb or some other source of quality protein. Keep the dog on this diet (with no additives) for a month. If the symptoms of food allergy or intolerance disappear, chances are your dog has a food allergy.

Don't think that the single

VITAL SIGNS

A dog's normal temperature is 101.5 degrees Fahrenheit. A range of between 100.0 and 102.5 degrees should be considered normal, as each dog's body sets its own temperature. It will be helpful if you take your dog's temperature when you know he is healthy and record it. Then, when you suspect that he is not feeling well, you will have a normal figure to compare the abnormal temperature against.

The normal pulse rate for a dog is between 100 and 125 beats per minute.

ingredient cured the problem. You still must find a suitable diet and ascertain which ingredient in the old diet was objectionable. This is most easily done by adding ingredients to the new diet one at a time. Let the dog stay on the modified diet for a month before you add another ingredient. Eventually, you will determine the ingredient that caused the adverse reaction.

An alternative method is to carefully study the ingredients in the diet to which your dog is allergic or intolerable. Identify the main ingredient in this diet and eliminate the main ingredient by buying a different food that does not have that ingredient. Keep experimenting until the symptoms disappear after one month on the new diet.

A male dog flea, *Ctenocephalides canis.*

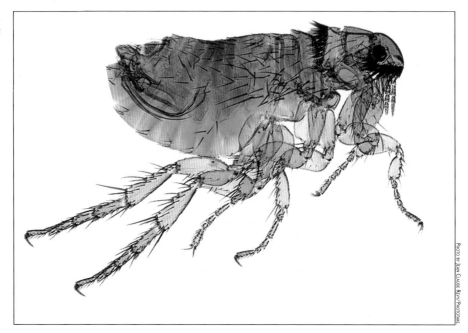

EXTERNAL PARASITES

FLEAS

Of all the problems to which dogs are prone, none is more well known and frustrating than fleas. Flea infestation is relatively simple to cure but difficult to prevent. Parasites that are harbored inside the body are a bit more difficult to eradicate but they are easier to control.

To control flea infestation, you have to understand the flea's life cycle. Fleas are often thought of as a summertime problem, but centrally heated homes have changed the patterns and fleas can be found at any time of the year. The most effective method of flea control is a two-stage approach: one stage to kill the adult fleas, and the other to control the development of pre-adult fleas. Unfortunately, no single active ingredient is effective against all stages of the life cycle.

FLEA KILLER CAUTION— "POISON"

Flea-killers are poisonous. You should not spray these toxic chemicals on areas of a dog's body that he licks, including his genitals and his face. Flea killers taken internally are a better answer, but check with your vet in case internal therapy is not advised for your dog.

LIFE CYCLE STAGES

During its life, a flea will pass through four life stages: egg, larva, pupa or nymph and adult. The adult stage is the most visible and irritating stage of the flea life cycle, and this is why the majority of flea-control products concentrate on this stage. The fact is that adult fleas account for only 1% of the total flea population, and the other 99% exist in pre-adult stages, i.e. eggs, larvae and nymphs. The pre-adult stages are barely visible to the naked eye.

THE LIFE CYCLE OF THE FLEA

Eggs are laid on the dog, usually in quantities of about 20 or 30, several times a day. The adult female flea must have a blood meal before each egg-laying session. When first laid, the eggs will cling to the dog's hair, as the eggs are still moist. However, they will quickly dry out and fall from the dog, especially if the dog moves around or scratches. Many eggs will fall off in the dog's favorite area or an area in which he spends a lot of time, such as his bed.

Once the eggs fall from the dog onto the carpet or furniture, they will hatch into larvae. This takes from one to ten days. Larvae are not particularly mobile and will usually travel only a few inches from where they hatch. However, they do have a tendency to move away from bright light and heavy

**EN GARDE:
CATCHING FLEAS OFF GUARD!**
Consider the following ways to arm yourself against fleas:
- Add a small amount of pennyroyal or eucalyptus oil to your dog's bath. These natural remedies repel fleas.
- Supplement your dog's food with fresh garlic (minced or grated) and a hearty amount of brewer's yeast, both of which ward off fleas.
- Use a flea comb on your dog daily. Submerge fleas in a cup of bleach to kill them quickly.
- Confine the dog to only a few rooms to limit the spread of fleas in the home.
- Vacuum daily...and get all of the crevices! Dispose of the bag every few days until the problem is under control.
- Wash your dog's bedding daily. Cover cushions where your dog sleeps with towels, and wash the towels often.

traffic—under furniture and behind doors are common places to find high quantities of flea larvae.

The flea larvae feed on dead organic matter, including adult flea feces, until they are ready to change into adult fleas. Fleas will usually remain as larvae for around seven days. After this period, the larvae will pupate into protective pupae. While inside the pupae, the larvae will undergo metamorphosis and change into adult fleas. This can take as little time as a few days, but the adult fleas can remain inside the pupae waiting to hatch for up to two years. The pupae are signaled to hatch by certain stimuli, such as physical pressure—the pupae's being stepped on, heat from an animal's lying on the pupae or increased carbon-dioxide levels and vibrations—indicating that a suitable host is available.

Once hatched, the adult flea must feed within a few days. Once the adult flea finds a host, it will not leave voluntarily. It only becomes dislodged by grooming or the host animal's scratching.

The adult flea will remain on the host for the duration of its life unless forcibly removed.

TREATING THE ENVIRONMENT AND THE DOG

Treating fleas should be a two-pronged attack. First, the environment needs to be treated; this includes carpets and furniture, especially the dog's bedding and areas underneath furniture. The environment should be treated with a household spray containing an Insect Growth Regulator (IGR) and an insecticide to kill the adult fleas. Most IGRs are effective against eggs and larvae; they actually mimic the fleas' own hormones and stop the eggs and larvae from developing into adult fleas. There are currently no treatments available to attack the pupa stage of the life cycle, so the adult insecticide is used to kill the newly hatched adult fleas before they find a host. Most IGRs are active for many months, while

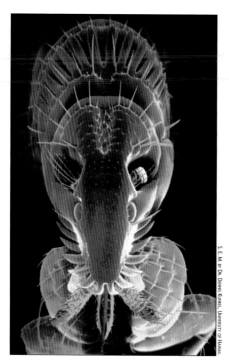

A scanning electron micrograph of a dog or cat flea, *Ctenocephalides*, magnified more than 100x. This image has been colorized for effect.

THE LIFE CYCLE OF THE FLEA

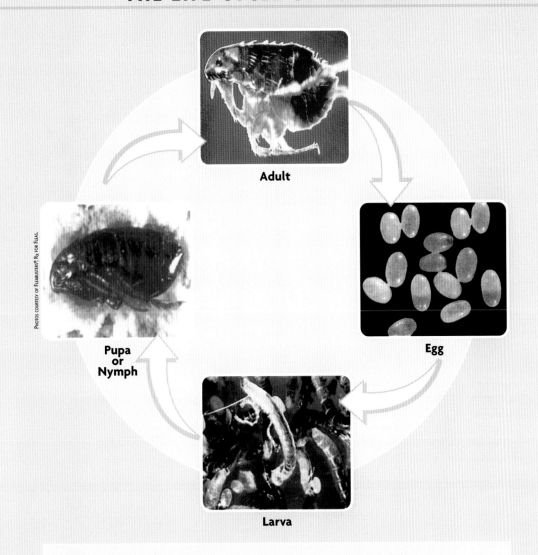

Adult

Egg

Larva

Pupa or Nymph

Fleas have been around for millions of years and have adapted to changing host animals. They are able to go through a complete life cycle in less than one month or they can extend their lives to almost two years by remaining as pupae or cocoons. They do not need blood or any other food for up to 20 months.

INSECT GROWTH REGULATOR (IGR)

Two types of products should be used when treating fleas—a product to treat the pet and a product to treat the home. Adult fleas represent less than 1% of the flea population. The pre-adult fleas (eggs, larvae and pupae) represent more than 99% of the flea population and are found in the environment; it is in the case of pre-adult fleas that products containing an Insect Growth Regulator (IGR) should be used in the home.

IGRs are a new class of compounds used to prevent the development of insects. They do not kill the insect outright, but instead use the insect's biology against it to stop it from completing its growth. Products that contain methoprene are the world's first and leading IGRs. Used to control fleas and other insects, this type of IGR will stop flea larvae from developing and protect the house for up to seven months.

The American dog tick, *Dermacentor variabilis*, is probably the most common tick found on dogs. Look at the strength in its eight legs! No wonder it's hard to detach them.

adult insecticides are only active for a few days.

When treating with a household spray, it is a good idea to vacuum before applying the product. This stimulates as many pupae as possible to hatch into adult fleas. The vacuum cleaner should also be treated with an insecticide to prevent the eggs and larvae that have been collected in the vacuum bag from hatching.

The second stage of treatment is to apply an adult insecticide to the dog. Traditionally, this would be in the form of a collar or a spray, but more recent innovations include digestible insecticides that poison the fleas when they ingest the dog's blood. Alternatively, there are drops that, when placed on the back of the dog's neck, spread throughout the hair and skin to kill adult fleas.

TICKS

Though not as common as fleas, ticks are found all over the tropical and temperate world. They don't bite, like fleas; they harpoon. They dig their sharp proboscis (nose) into the dog's skin and drink the blood. Their

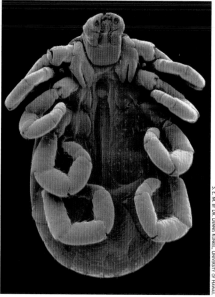

only food and drink is dog's blood. Dogs can get Lyme disease, Rocky Mountain spotted fever, tick bite paralysis and many other diseases from ticks. They may live where fleas are found and they like to hide in cracks or seams in walls. They are controlled the same way fleas are controlled.

The American dog tick, *Dermacentor variabilis*, may well be the most common dog tick in many geographical areas, especially those areas where the climate is hot and humid. Most dog ticks have life expectancies of a week to six months, depending upon climatic conditions. They can neither jump nor fly, but they can crawl slowly and can range up to 16 feet to reach a sleeping or unsuspecting dog.

MITES

Just as fleas and ticks can be problematic for your dog, mites can also lead to an itchy nuisance. Microscopic in size, mites are related to ticks and generally take up permanent residence on their host animal—in this case, your dog! The term *mange* refers to any infestation caused by one of the mighty mites, of which there are six varieties that concern dog owners.

Demodex mites cause a condition known as demodicosis

DEER-TICK CROSSING
The great outdoors may be fun for your dog, but it also is an home to dangerous ticks. Deer ticks carry a bacterium known as *Borrelia burgdorferi* and are most active in the autumn and spring. When infections are caught early, penicillin and tetracycline are effective antibiotics, but if left untreated the bacteria may cause neurological, kidney and cardiac problems as well as long-term trouble with walking and painful joints.

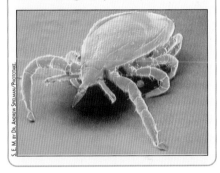

S. E. M. BY DR. ANDREW SPIELMAN/PHOTOTAKE.

PHOTO BY DR. DENNIS KUNKEL, UNIVERSITY OF HAWAII.

The head of an American dog tick, *Dermacentor variabilis*, enlarged and colorized for effect.

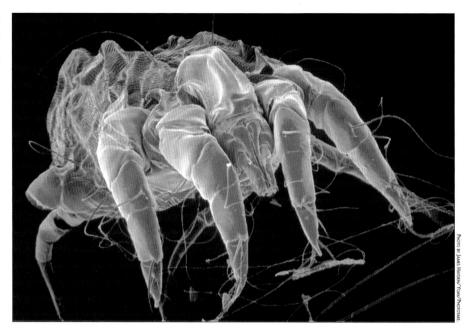

The mange mite, *Psoroptes bovis*, can infest cattle and other domestic animals.

(sometimes called red mange or follicular mange), in which the mites live in the dog's hair follicles and sebaceous glands in larger-than-normal amounts. This type of mange is commonly passed from the dam to her puppies and usually shows up on the puppies' muzzles, though demodicosis is not transferable from one normal dog to another. Most dogs recover from this type of mange without any treatment, though topical therapies are commonly prescribed by the vet.

The *Cheyletiellosis* mite is the hook-mouthed culprit associated with "walking dandruff," a condition that affects dogs as well as cats and rabbits. This mite lives on the surface of the animal's skin and is readily transferable through direct or indirect contact with an affected animal. The dandruff is present in the form of scaly skin, which may or may not be itchy. If not treated, this mange can affect a whole kennel of dogs and can be spread to humans as well.

The *Sarcoptes* mite causes intense itching on the dog in the form of a condition known as scabies or sarcoptic mange. The cycle of the *Sarcoptes* mite lasts about three weeks, and the mites live in the top layer of the dog's skin (epidermis), preferably in

Human lice look like dog lice; the two are closely related.

areas with little hair. Scabies is highly contagious and can be passed to humans. Sometimes an allergic reaction to the mite worsens the severe itching associated with sarcoptic mange.

Ear mites, *Otodectes cynotis,* lead to otodectic mange, which most commonly affects the outer ear canal of the dog, though other areas can be affected as well. Dogs with ear-mite infestation commonly scratch at their ears, causing further irritation, and shake their heads. Dark brown droppings in the outer ear confirm the diagnosis. Your vet can prescribe a treatment to flush out the ears and kill any eggs in the ears. A complete month of treatment is necessary to cure the mange.

Two other mites, less common in dogs, include *Dermanyssus gallinae* (the poultry or red mite) and *Eutrombicula alfreddugesi* (the North American mite associated with trombiculidiasis or chigger infestation). The poultry mite frequently lives on chickens, but can transfer to dogs who spend time near farm animals. Chigger infestation affects dogs in the

> ### DO NOT MIX
> Never mix parasite-control products without first consulting your vet. Some products can become toxic when combined with others and can cause fatal consequences.

> ### NOT A DROP TO DRINK
> Never allow your dog to swim in polluted water or public areas where water quality can be suspect. Even perfectly clear water can harbor parasites, many of which can cause serious to fatal illnesses in canines. Areas inhabited by water-fowl and other wildlife are especially dangerous.

Central US who have exposure to woodlands. The types of mange caused by both of these mites are treatable by veterinarians.

INTERNAL PARASITES
Most animals—fishes, birds and mammals, including dogs and humans—have worms and other parasites that live inside their bodies. According to Dr. Herbert R. Axelrod, the fish pathologist, there are two kinds of parasites: dumb and smart. The smart parasites live in peaceful cooperation with their hosts (symbiosis), while the dumb parasites kill their hosts. Most worm infections are relatively easy to control. If they are not controlled, they weaken the host dog to the point that other medical problems occur, but they do not kill the host as dumb parasites would.

The brown dog tick, *Rhipicephalus sanguineus*, is an uncommon but annoying tick found on dogs.

PHOTO BY CAROLINA BIOLOGICAL SUPPLY/PHOTOTAKE.

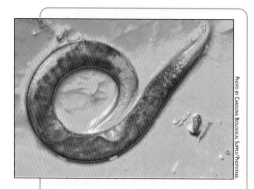

PHOTO BY CAROLINA BIOLOGICAL SUPPLY/PHOTOTAKE

The roundworm *Rhabditis* can infect both dogs and humans.

The roundworm, *Ascaris lumbricoides*.

ROUNDWORMS

Average-size dogs can pass 1,360,000 roundworm eggs every day. For example, if there were only 1 million dogs in the world, the world would be saturated with thousands of tons of dog feces. These feces would contain around 15,000,000,000 roundworm eggs.

Up to 31% of home yards and children's sand boxes in the US contain roundworm eggs.

Flushing dog's feces down the toilet is not a safe practice because the usual sewage treatments do not destroy roundworm eggs.

Infected puppies start shedding roundworm eggs at three weeks of age. They can be infected by their mother's milk.

ROUNDWORMS

The roundworms that infect dogs are known scientifically as *Toxocara canis.* They live in the dog's intestines and shed eggs continually. It has been estimated that a dog produces about 6 or more ounces of feces every day. Each ounce of feces averages hundreds of thousands of roundworm eggs. There are no known areas in which dogs roam that do not contain roundworm eggs. The greatest danger of roundworms is that they infect people, too! It is wise to have your dog tested regularly for roundworms.

In young puppies, roundworms cause bloated bellies, diarrhea, coughing and vomiting, and are transmitted from the dam (through blood or milk). Affected puppies will not appear as animated as normal puppies. The worms appear spaghetti-like, measuring as long as 6 inches. Adult dogs can acquire roundworms through coprophagia (eating contaminated feces) or by killing rodents that carry roundworms.

Roundworm infection can kill puppies and cause severe problems in adults, as the hatched larvae travel to the lungs and trachea through the bloodstream. Cleanliness is the best preventative for roundworms. Always pick up after your dog and dispose of feces in appropriate receptacles.

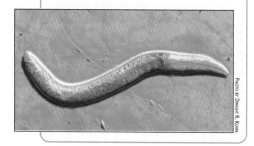

PHOTO BY DWIGHT R. KUHN.

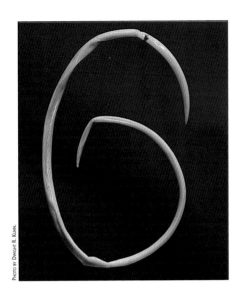

PHOTO BY DWIGHT R. KUHN.

HOOKWORMS

In the United States, dog owners have to be concerned about four different species of hookworm, the most common and most serious of which is *Ancylostoma caninum,* which prefers warm climates. The others are *Ancylostoma braziliense, Ancylostoma tubaeforme* and *Uncinaria stenocephala,* the latter of which is a concern to dogs living in the Northern US and Canada, as this species prefers cold climates. Hookworms are dangerous to humans as well as to dogs and cats, and can be the cause of severe anemia due to iron deficiency. The worm uses its teeth to attach itself to the dog's intestines and changes the site of its attachment about six times per day. Each time the worm repositions itself, the dog loses

blood and can become anemic. *Ancylostoma caninum* is the most likely of the four species to cause anemia in the dog.

Symptoms of hookworm infection include dark stools, weight loss, general weakness, pale coloration and anemia, as well as possible skin problems. Fortunately, hookworms are easily purged from the affected dog with a number of medications that have proven effective. Discuss these with your veterinarian. Most heartworm preventatives include a hookworm insecticide as well.

Owners also must be aware that hookworms can infect humans, who can acquire the larvae through exposure to contaminated feces. Since the worms cannot complete their life cycle on a human, the worms simply infest the skin and cause irritation. This condition is known as cutaneous larva migrans syndrome. As a preventative, use disposable gloves or a "poop-scoop" to pick up your dog's droppings and prevent your dog (or neighborhood cats) from defecating in children's play areas.

The hookworm, *Ancylostoma caninum.*

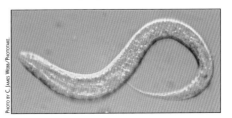

PHOTO BY C. JAMES WEBB/PHOTOTAKE.

The infective stage of the hookworm larva.

TAPEWORMS

Humans, rats, squirrels, foxes, coyotes, wolves and domestic dogs are all susceptible to tapeworm infection. Except in humans, tapeworms are usually not a fatal infection. Infected individuals can harbor 1000 parasitic worms.

Tapeworms, like some other types of worm, are hermaphroditic, meaning male and female in the same worm.

If dogs eat infected rats or mice, or anything else infected with tapeworm, they get the tapeworm disease. One month after attaching to a dog's intestine, the worm starts shedding eggs. These eggs are infective immediately. Infective eggs can live for a few months without a host animal.

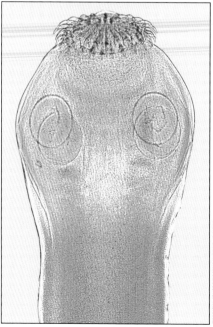

The head and rostellum (the round prominence on the scolex) of a tapeworm, which infects dogs and humans.

PHOTO BY CAROLINA BIOLOGICAL SUPPLY/PHOTOTAKE

TAPEWORMS

There are many species of tapeworm, all of which are carried by fleas! The most common tapeworm affecting dogs is known as *Dipylidium caninum*. The dog eats the flea and starts the tapeworm cycle. Humans can also be infected with tapeworms—so don't eat fleas! Fleas are so small that your dog could pass them onto your hands, your plate or your food and thus make it possible for you to ingest a flea that is carrying tapeworm eggs.

While tapeworm infection is not life-threatening in dogs (smart parasite!), it can be the cause of a very serious liver disease for humans. About 50% of the humans infected with *Echinococcus multilocularis*, a type of tapeworm that causes alveolar hydatid, perish.

WHIPWORMS

In North America, whipworms are counted among the most common parasitic worms in dogs. The whipworm's scientific name is *Trichuris vulpis*. These worms attach themselves in the lower parts of the intestine, where they feed. Affected dogs may only experience upset tummies, colic and diarrhea. These worms, however, can live for months or years in the dog, beginning their larval stage in the small intestine, spending their adult stage in the large intestine and finally passing infective eggs through the dog's feces. The only way to detect whipworms is through a fecal examination, though this is not always foolproof. Treatment for whipworms is tricky, due to the worms' unusual life-cycle pattern, and very often dogs are reinfected due to exposure to infective eggs on the ground. The whipworm eggs can survive in the environment for as long as five years, thus cleaning up droppings in your own backyard as well as in public places is absolutely essential for sanitation purposes and the health of your dog and others.

THREADWORMS

Though less common than roundworms, hookworms and those already mentioned, threadworms concern dog owners in the Southwestern US and Gulf Coast area where the climate is hot and humid. Living in the small intestine of the dog, this worm measures a mere 2 millimeters and is round in shape. Like that of the whipworm, the threadworm's life cycle is very complex and the eggs and larvae are passed through the feces. A deadly disease in humans, *Strongyloides* readily infects people, and the handling of feces is the most common means of transmission. Threadworms are most often seen in young puppies; bloody diarrhea and pneumonia are symptoms. Sick puppies must be isolated and treated immediately; vets recommend a follow-up treatment one month later.

HEARTWORM PREVENTATIVES

There are many heartworm preventatives on the market, many of which are sold at your veterinarian's office. These products can be given daily or monthly, depending on the manufacturer's instructions. All of these preventatives contain chemical insecticides directed at killing heartworms, which leads to some controversy among dog owners. In effect, heartworm preventatives are necessary evils, though you should determine how necessary based on your pet's lifestyle. There is no doubt that heartworm is a dreadful disease that threatens the lives of dogs. However, the likelihood of your dog's being bitten by an infected mosquito is slim in most places, and a mosquito-repellent (or an herbal remedy such as Wormwood or Black Walnut) is much safer for your dog and will not compromise his immune system (the way heartworm preventatives will). Should you decide to use the traditional preventative "medications," you can consider giving the pill every other or third month. Since the toxins in the pill will kill the heartworms at all stages of development, the pill would be effective in killing larvae, nymphs or adults and it takes four months for the larvae to reach the adult stage. Thus, there is no rationale to poisoning the dog's system on a monthly basis. Lastly, do not give the pill during the winter months since there are no mosquitoes around to pass on their infection, unless you live in a tropical environment.

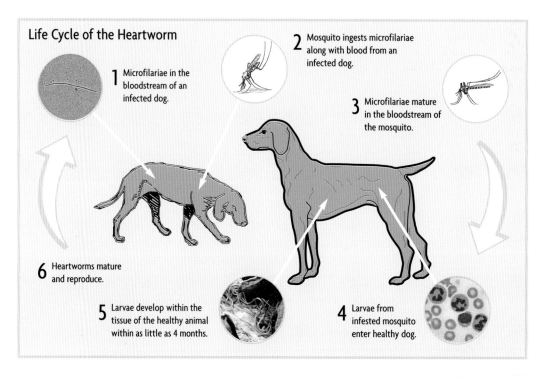

Life Cycle of the Heartworm

1 Microfilariae in the bloodstream of an infected dog.

2 Mosquito ingests microfilariae along with blood from an infected dog.

3 Microfilariae mature in the bloodstream of the mosquito.

4 Larvae from infested mosquito enter healthy dog.

5 Larvae develop within the tissue of the healthy animal within as little as 4 months.

6 Heartworms mature and reproduce.

HEARTWORMS

Heartworms are thin, extended worms up to 12 inches long, which live in a dog's heart and the major blood vessels surrounding it. Dogs may have up to 200 worms. Symptoms may be loss of energy, loss of appetite, coughing, the development of a pot belly and anemia.

Heartworms are transmitted by mosquitoes. The mosquito drinks the blood of an infected dog and takes in larvae with the blood. The larvae, called microfilariae, develop within the body of the mosquito and are passed on to the next dog bitten after the larvae

mature. It takes two to three weeks for the larvae to develop to the infective stage within the body of the mosquito. Dogs are usually treated at about six weeks of age and maintained on a prophylactic dose given monthly.

Blood testing for heartworms is not necessarily indicative of how seriously your dog is infected. Although this is a dangerous disease, it is not easy for a dog to be infected. Discuss the various preventatives with your vet, as there are many different types now available. Together you can decide on a safe course of prevention for your dog.

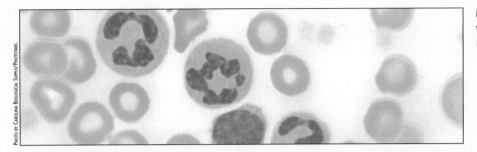

Magnified heart-worm larvae, *Diro-filaria immitis.*

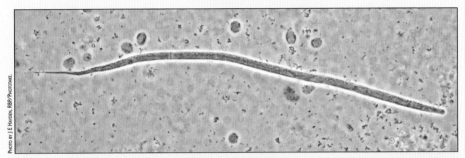

Heartworm, *Diro-filaria immitis.*

The heart of a dog infected with canine heart-worm, *Dirofilaria immitis.*

HOMEOPATHY:
an alternative
to conventional
medicine

"Less is Most'"

Using this principle, the strength of a homeopathic remedy is measured by the number of serial dilutions that were undertaken to create it. The greater the number of serial dilutions, the greater the strength of the homeopathic remedy. The potency of a remedy that has been made by making a dilution of 1 part in 100 parts (or 1/100) is 1c or 1cH. If this remedy is subjected to a series of further dilutions, each one being 1/100, a more dilute and stronger remedy is produced. If the remedy is diluted in this way six times, it is called 6c or 6cH. A dilution of 6c is 1 part in 1,000,000,000,000. In general, higher potencies in more frequent doses are better for acute symptoms and lower potencies in more infrequent doses are more useful for chronic, long-standing problems.

CURING YOUR DOG NATURALLY

Holistic medicine means treating the whole animal as a unique, perfect living being. Generally, holistic treatments do not suppress the symptoms that the body naturally produces, as do most medications prescribed by conventional doctors and vets. Holistic methods seek to cure disease by regaining balance and harmony in the patient's environment. Some of these methods include use of nutritional therapy, herbs, flower essences, aromatherapy, acupuncture, massage, chiropractic and, of course the most popular holistic approach, homeopathy.

Homeopathy is a theory or system of treating illness with small doses of substances which, if administered in larger quantities, would produce the symptoms that the patient already has. This approach is often described as "like cures like." Although modern veterinary medicine is geared toward the "quick fix," homeopathy relies on the belief that, given the time, the body is able to heal itself and return to its natural, healthy state.

Choosing a remedy to cure a problem in our dogs is the difficult part of homeopathy. Consult with your veterinarian for a professional diagnosis of your dog's symptoms. Often these symptoms require immediate conventional care. If your vet is willing, and knowledgeable, you may attempt a homeopathic remedy. Be aware that cortisone prevents homeopathic remedies from working. There are hundreds of possibilities and combinations to cure many problems in dogs, from basic physical problems such as excessive shedding, fleas or other parasites, unattractive doggy odor, bad breath, upset stomach, obesity, dry, oily or dull coat, diarrhea, ear problems or eye discharge (including tears and dry or mucousy matter), to behavioral abnormalities such as fear of loud noises, habitual licking, poor appetite, excessive barking and various phobias. From alumina to zincum metallicum, the remedies span the planet and the imagination...from flowers and weeds to chemicals, insect droppings, diesel smoke and volcanic ash.

Using "Like to Treat Like"

Unlike conventional medicines that suppress symptoms, homeopathic remedies treat illnesses with small doses of substances that, if administered in larger quantities, would produce the symptoms that the patient already has. While the same homeopathic remedy can be used to treat different symptoms in different dogs, here are some interesting remedies and their uses.

Apis Mellifica
(made from honey bee venom) can be used for allergies or to reduce swelling that occurs in acutely infected kidneys.

Diesel Smoke
can be used to help control motion sickness.

Calcarea Fluorica
(made from calcium fluoride, which helps harden bone structure) can be useful in treating hard lumps in tissues.

Natrum Muriaticum
(made from common salt, sodium chloride) is useful in treating thin, thirsty dogs.

Nitricum Acidum
(made from nitric acid) is used for symptoms you would expect to see from contact with acids, such as lesions, especially where the skin joins the linings of body orifices or openings such as the lips and nostrils.

Symphytum
(made from the herb Knitbone, *Symphytum officianale)* is used to encourage bones to heal.

Urtica Urens
(made from the common stinging nettle) is used in treating painful, irritating rashes.

Showing Your
LHASA APSO

Floating around the show ring, this Lhasa is showing the he has what it takes to do big winning in the ring!

When you purchase your Lhasa Apso, you will make it clear to the breeder whether you want one just as a lovable companion and pet, or if you hope to be buying a Lhasa Apso with show prospects. No reputable breeder will sell you a young puppy and tell you that he is *definitely* of show quality, for so much can go wrong during the early months of a puppy's development. If you plan to show, what you will hopefully have acquired is a puppy with "show potential."

To the novice, exhibiting a Lhasa Apso in the show ring may look easy, but it takes a lot of hard work and devotion to do top winning at a show such as the prestigious Westminster Kennel Club dog show, not to mention a little luck too!

The first concept that the canine novice learns when watch-

ing a dog show is that each dog first competes against members of his own breed. Once the judge has selected the best member of each breed (Best of Breed), provided that the show is judged on a Group system, that chosen dog will compete with other Best of Breed dogs in his group. Finally, the dogs chosen first in each group will compete for Best in Show.

The second concept that you must understand is that the dogs are not actually compared against one another. The judge compares each dog against his breed standard, the approved word depiction of the ideal specimen that is approved by the American Kennel Club (AKC). While some early breed standards were indeed based on specific dogs that were famous or popular, many dedicated enthusiasts say that a perfect specimen, as described in the standard, has never walked into a show ring, has never been

AKC GROUPS

For showing purposes, the American Kennel Club divides its recognized breeds into seven groups: Non-Sporting Dogs (to which the Lhasa Apso belongs), Hounds, Working Dogs, Terriers, Toys, Sporting Dogs and Herding Dogs.

bred and, to the woe of dog breeders around the globe, does not exist. Breeders attempt to get as close to this ideal as possible with every litter, but theoretically the "perfect" dog is so elusive that it is impossible. (And if the "perfect" dog were born, breeders and judges would never agree that it was indeed "perfect.")

If you are interested in exploring the world of dog showing, your best bet is to join your local breed club or the national parent club, which is the American Lhasa Apso Club. These clubs often host both regional and national specialties, shows only for Lhasa Apsos, which can include conformation as well as obedience and agility trials. Even if you have no intention of competing with your Lhasa Apso, a specialty is like a festival for lovers of the breed who congregate to share their favorite topic: the Lhasa Apso! Clubs also send out newsletters, and some organize training days and seminars in order that people may learn more about their chosen breed. To locate the breed club closest to you, contact the American Kennel Club, which furnishes the rules and regulations for all of these events plus general dog registration and other basic requirements of dog ownership.

The American Kennel Club offers three kinds of conformation shows: an all-breed show (for all

AKC-recognized breeds), a specialty show (for one breed only, usually sponsored by the parent club) and a Group show (for all breeds in the Group).

For a dog to become an AKC champion of record, the dog must accumulate 15 points at the shows from at least three different judges, including two "majors." A "major"

BECOMING A CHAMPION

An official AKC champion of record requires that a dog accumulate 15 points under three different judges, including two "majors" under different judges. Points are awarded based on the number of dogs entered into competition, varying from breed to breed and place to place. A win of three, four or five points is considered a "major." The AKC annually assigns a schedule of points to adjust to the variations that accompany a breed's popularity and the population of a given area.

is defined as a three-, four- or five-point win, and the number of points per win is determined by the number of dogs entered in the show on that day. Depending on the breed, the number of points that are awarded varies. In a breed as popular as the Lhasa Apso, more dogs are needed to rack up the points. At any dog show, only one dog and one bitch of each breed can win points.

Dog showing does not offer "co-ed" classes. Dogs and bitches never compete against each other in the classes. Non-champion dogs are called "class dogs" because they compete in one of five classes. Dogs are entered in a particular class depending on age and previous show wins. To begin, there is the Puppy Class (for 6- to 9-month-olds and for 9- to 12-month-olds); this class is followed by the Novice Class (for dogs that have not won any first prizes except in the Puppy Class or three first prizes in the Novice Class and have not accumulated any points toward their champion title); the Bred-by-Exhibitor Class (for dogs handled by their breeders or handled by one of the breeder's immediate family); the American-bred Class (for dogs bred in the US); and the Open Class (for any dog that is not a champion).

The judge at the show begins judging the Puppy Class, first dogs and then bitches, and proceeds through the classes. The judge places his winners first through fourth in each class. In the Winners Class, the first-place winners of each class compete with one another to determine Winners Dog and Winners Bitch. The judge also places a Reserve Winners Dog and Reserve Winners Bitch, which could be awarded the points in the case of a disqualification. The Winners Dog and Winners Bitch are the two that are awarded the points for the breed; they then compete with any champions of record entered in the show (known as "specials"). The judge reviews the Winners

SHOW-RING ETIQUETTE

Just as with anything else, there is a certain etiquette to the show ring that can only be learned through experience. Showing your dog can be quite intimidating to you as a novice when it seems as if everyone else knows what he is doing. You can familiarize yourself with ring procedure beforehand by taking showing classes to prepare you and your dog for conformation showing and by talking with experienced handlers. When you are in the ring, it is very important to pay attention and listen to the instructions you are given by the judge about where to move your dog. Remember, even the most skilled handlers had to start somewhere. Keep it up and you too will become a proficient handler as you gain practice and experience.

Dog, Winners Bitch and all of the "specials" to select his Best of Breed. The Best of Winners is selected between the Winners Dog and Winners Bitch. Were one of these two to be selected Best of Breed, he would automatically be named Best of Winners as well. Finally the judge selects his Best of Opposite Sex to the Best of Breed winner.

At a Group show or all-breed show, the Best of Breed winners from each breed then compete against one another for Group One through Group Four. The judge compares each Best of Breed to his breed standard, and the dog that most closely lives up to the ideal for his breed is selected as Group One. Finally, all seven group winners (from the Non-Sporting Group, Toy Group, Hound Group, etc.) compete for Best in Show.

To find out about dog shows in your area, you can subscribe to the American Kennel Club's monthly magazine, the *American Kennel Gazette* and the accompanying *Events Calendar*. You can also look in your local newspaper for advertisements for dog shows in your area or go on the Internet to the AKC's website, www.akc.org.

If your Lhasa Apso is six months of age or older and registered with the AKC, you can enter him in a dog show where the breed is offered classes. Provided that your Lhasa Apso does not

have a disqualifying fault, he can compete. Only unaltered dogs can be entered in a dog show, so if you have spayed or neutered your Lhasa Apso, your dog cannot compete in conformation shows. The reason for this is simple. Dog shows are the main forum to prove which representatives in a breed are worthy of being bred. Only dogs that have achieved championships—the AKC "seal of approval" for quality in pure-bred dogs—-should be bred. Altered dogs, however, can participate in other AKC events such as obedience trials and the Canine Good Citizen® program.

There is a lot of anticipation as Lhasa Apsos are prepared for their turn in the ring at an outdoor breed show in Australia.

HANDLING

Before you actually step into the ring, you would be well advised to sit back and observe the judge's ring procedure. If it is your first time in the ring, do not be over-anxious. It is much better to stand back and study how the exhibitor in front of you is performing. The judge asks each handler to "stack" the dog, hopefully showing the dog off to his best advantage. The judge will observe the dog from a distance and from different angles, and approach the dog to check his teeth, overall structure, alertness and muscle tone, as well as consider how well the dog "conforms" to the standard. Most importantly, the judge will have the exhibitor move the dog around the ring in some pattern that he should specify (always listen since some judges change their directions—and the judge is always right!). Finally, the judge will give the dog one last look

before moving on to the next exhibitor.

If you are not in the top four in your class at your first show, do not be discouraged. Be patient and consistent, and you may eventually find yourself in a winning line-up. Remember that the winners were once in your shoes and have devoted many hours and much money to earn the placement. If you find that your dog is losing every time and never getting a nod, it may be time to consider a different dog sport or to just enjoy your Lhasa Apso as a pet. Parent clubs offer other events, such as agility, track-ing, obedience, instinct tests and more, which may be of interest to the owner of a well-trained Lhasa Apso.

OBEDIENCE TRIALS

Obedience trials in the US trace back to the early 1930s when organized obedience training was developed to demonstrate how well dog and owner could work together. The pioneer of obedience trials is Mrs. Helen Whitehouse Walker, a Standard Poodle fancier, who designed a series of exercises after the Associated Sheep, Police Army Dog Society of Great Britain. Since the early days, obedience trials have grown by leaps and bounds, and today there are over 2,000 trials held in the US every year, with more than 100,000 dogs competing. Any

PRACTICE AT HOME

If you have decided to show your dog, you must train him to gait around the ring by your side at the correct pace and pattern, and to tolerate being handled and examined by the judge. Most breeds require complete denti-tion, all breeds require a particular bite (scissors, level or undershot) and all males must have two apparently normal testicles fully descended into the scrotum. Enlist family and friends to hold mock trials in your yard to prepare your future champion!

AKC-registered dog can enter an obedience trial, regardless of conformational disqualifications or neutering.

Obedience trials are divided into three levels of progressive difficulty. At the first level, the Novice, dogs compete for the title Companion Dog (CD); at the intermediate level, the Open, dogs compete for the title Companion Dog Excellent (CDX); and at the advanced level, the Utility, dogs compete for the title Utility Dog (UD). Classes are sub-divided into "A" (for beginners) and "B" (for more experienced handlers). A perfect score at any level is 200, and a dog must score 170 or better to earn a "leg," of which three are needed to earn the title. To earn points, the dog must score more than 50% of the available points in each exercise; the possible points range from 20 to 40.

Each level consists of a different set of exercises. In the Novice level, the dog must heel on- and off-leash, come, long sit, long down and stand for examination. These skills are the basic ones required for a well-behaved "Companion Dog." The Open level requires that the dog perform the same exercises above but without a leash for extended lengths of time, as well as retrieve a dumbbell, broad jump and drop on recall. In the Utility level, dogs must perform ten difficult exercises, including scent discrimina-

Best in Show winner at Tibethund, held in Sweden, judged by the author.

tion, hand signals for basic commands, directed jump and directed retrieve.

Once a dog has earned the UD title, he can compete with other proven obedience dogs for the

INFORMATION ON CLUBS

You can get information about dog shows from the national kennel clubs:

American Kennel Club
5580 Centerview Dr., Raleigh, NC 27606-3390
www.akc.org

United Kennel Club
100 E. Kilgore Road, Kalamazoo, MI 49002
www.ukcdogs.com

Canadian Kennel Club
89 Skyway Ave., Suite 100, Etobicoke, Ontario
M9W 6R4 Canada
www.ckc.ca

The Kennel Club
1-5 Clarges St., Piccadilly, London W1Y 8AB, UK
www.the-kennel-club.org.uk

coveted title of Utility Dog Excellent (UDX), which requires that the dog win "legs" in ten shows. Utility Dogs who earn "legs" in Open B and Utility B earn points toward their Obedience Trial Champion title. In 1977, the title Obedience Trial Champion (OTCh.) was established by the AKC. To become an OTCh., a dog needs to earn 100 points, which requires three first places in Open B and Utility under three different judges.

The Grand Prix of obedience trials, the AKC National Obedi-

ence Invitational gives qualifying Utility Dogs the chance to win the newest and highest title: National Obedience Champion (NOC). Only the top 25 ranked obedience dogs, plus any dog ranked in the top 3 in his breed, are allowed to compete.

TRACKING

Any dog is capable of tracking, using his nose to follow a trail. Tracking tests are exciting and competitive ways to test your Lhasa Apso's instinctive scenting ability. The AKC started tracking tests in 1937, when the first AKC-licensed test took place as part of the Utility level at an obedience trial. Ten years later in 1947, the AKC offered the first title, Tracking Dog (TD). It was not until 1980 that the AKC added the title Tracking Dog Excellent (TDX), which was followed by the title Versatile Surface Tracking (VST) in 1995. The title Champion Tracker (CT) is awarded to a dog who has earned all three titles.

In the beginning level of tracking, the owner follows the dog through a field on a long lead. To earn the TD title, the dog must follow a track laid by a human 30 to 120 minutes prior. The track is about 500 yards long with up to 5 directional changes. The TDX requires that the dog follow a track that is 3 to 5 hours old over a course up to 1,000 yards long with up to 7 directional changes.

MEET THE AKC

The American Kennel Club is the main governing body of the dog sport in the United States. Founded in 1884, the AKC consists of 500 or more independent dog clubs plus 4,500 affiliate clubs, all of which follow the AKC rules and regulations. Additionally, the AKC maintains a registry for pure-bred dogs in the US and works to preserve the integrity of the sport and its continuation in the country. Over 1,000,000 dogs are registered each year, representing about 150 recognized breeds. There are over 15,000 competitive events held annually for which over 2,000,000 dogs enter to participate. Dogs compete to earn over 40 different titles, from Champion to Companion Dog to Master Agility Champion.

This is what it is all about. A magnificent award-winning dog brings a great deal of personal satisfaction and pride to the show dog owner.

The VST requires that the dog follow a track up to 5 hours old through an urban setting.

AGILITY TRIALS
Having had its origins in the UK back in 1977, AKC agility had its official beginning in the US in August 1994, when the first licensed agility trials were held. The AKC allows all registered breeds (including Miscellaneous Class breeds) to participate, providing the dog is 12 months of age or older. Agility is designed so that the handler demonstrates how well the dog can work at his side. The handler directs his dog over an obstacle course that includes jumps as well as tires, the dog walk, weave poles, pipe tunnels, collapsed tunnels, etc. While working his way through

the course, the dog must keep one eye and ear on the handler and the rest of his body on the course. The handler gives verbal and hand signals to guide the dog through the course.

The first organization to promote agility trials in the US was the United States Dog Agility Association, Inc. (USDAA), which was established in 1986 and spawned numerous member clubs around the country. Both the USDAA and the AKC offer titles to winning dogs.

Agility is great fun for dog and owner with many rewards for everyone involved. Interested owners should join a training club that has obstacles and experienced agility handlers who can introduce you and your dog to the "ropes" (and tires, tunnels, etc.).

INDEX

My Lhasa Apso

PUT YOUR PUPPY'S FIRST PICTURE HERE

Dog's Name _____

Date _____ Photographer _____